LUIGI GUICCIARDINI

THE SACK OF ROME

LUIGI GUICCIARDINI

THE SACK OF ROME

TRANSLATED WITH AN INTRODUCTION
AND NOTES BY
JAMES H. MC GREGOR

ITALICA PRESS
NEW YORK
1993

ITALICA PRESS, INC.
595 Main Street
New York, New York 10044

Library of Congress Cataloging-in-Publication Data

Guicciardini, Luigi, 1478-1551.
    [Historia del sacco di Roma.   English]
    The sack of Rome / Luigi Guicciardini ; translated with an introduction and notes by James H. Mc Gregor.
        p.   cm.
    Includes bibliographical references (p. 133-137).
    ISBN 0-934977-32-1 : $10.00
    1. Rome (Italy)--History--Siege, 1527. I. Mc Gregor, James H. (James Harvey), 1946-   . II. Title.
DG812.12.G85 1992
945'.63206--dc20   92-38776
                                                                CIP

Printed in the United States of America
5 4 3 2 1

About the Editor:

James H. Mc Gregor is an associate professor of comparative literature at the University of Georgia. He has written two books on Giovanni Boccaccio that focus on the Italian author's classicism, historicism, and imitation of Vergil. He was awarded a Rome Prize Fellowship in Post-Classical Humanistic Studies at the American Academy in Rome in 1981-82; in 1984-85 he was a Visiting Professor of Italian at Berkeley. He is currently gathering materials for a book on Giovanni de' Medici and his family.

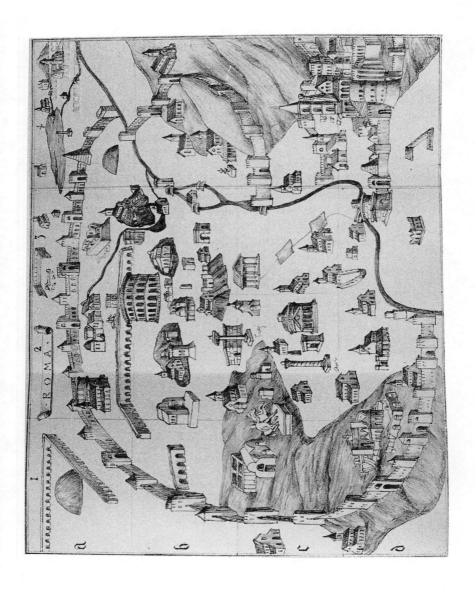

CONTENTS

ILLUSTRATIONS

PREFACE

S THE FIVE-HUNDREDTH ANNIVERSARY of Columbus' arrival in the Western Hemisphere approached, I found myself increasingly preoccupied with the notion that events in the New World were Renaissance events. Since there is little relationship between the massacre of indigenous peoples in Mexico and Michelangelo's decoration of the Sistine Chapel, however, we tend to ignore the fact that these events overlap in time. There is a thread of events that runs through the entire period of the High Renaissance in Italy that ties its fortunes very closely to those of the New World. In the decade of Columbus' first voyages, a series of wars and invasions began in Italy that lasted for more than thirty years. This series of internecine and international wars culminated in 1527 in the invasion, sack, and occupation of the city of Rome.

Spanish and German troops of the Emperor Charles V carried out that invasion and sack. Spanish troops of the same emperor also raped, murdered, and tortured the Aztecs and Incas, and pillaged and burned their cities. The horrors visited on the New World were not unique to our hemisphere. Spanish troops did not throw away the rule book and run amok when they left Europe behind. They brought the common culture and practices of soldiers, officers, and political leaders with them to this hemisphere. What happened in Tenochtitlán in 1521 happened again in Rome in 1527. The Aztec emperor and

Pope Clement VII faced equal violence and may have been menaced by some of the very same soldiers.

In researching the sack of Rome, I came upon Luigi Guicciardini's text. It exists in a single "modern" Italian edition of 1867. It has not been translated before. The picture it presents of the political situation that culminated in the sack is clear and insightful. It gives a vivid sense of the personalities involved in the war that led to the sack. It does not flinch from showing the devastation and degradation experienced by men and women in the capital of Christianity.

In preparing this edition of Luigi's text, I have tried to aid the modern reader while preserving the integrity of the original. My introduction describes the author and gives some sense of his qualifications and point of view. It sets the scene for the events leading up to the formation of an alliance against Emperor Charles V, which Luigi takes as the beginning point of his history. That alliance was formed in 1526; and Luigi probably started writing soon after it was signed. By and large his reference point in the text is contemporary with the events he narrates; he ends his account sometime in the summer of 1527. My introduction is followed by a letter of dedication. Luigi dedicated his history to Cosimo de' Medici, who began ruling Florence in 1537. This dedicatory letter, which introduces some of Luigi's major themes, is the only part of the text, I believe, that was added after 1527.

I have taken a slight liberty with the text by labeling the next section a Prologue. It serves that purpose, although it does not bear that name in the original. In it Luigi alludes to the background events I have described more fully in my introduction. The two books of the history are transcribed without editorial intrusion. I have broken up Luigi's long and often complicated sentences and I have shortened his paragraphs. I have kept his deferential forms of reference including his use of the expression "Our Lord," to refer to the pope. I have translated his method of time keeping, which is based on a twenty-four hour clock that begins at sunset each day, into the American twelve-hour clock. In referring to years he always drops the designation of the century and I have followed this usage. I have used the modern spelling for Italian place names to avoid confusion, despite the occasional anachronism that involves (e.g. Luigi's Sasso is now called Sasso Marconi in honor of the inventor of radio).

The text is accompanied by three maps. One depicts northern Italy, the scene of the first wave of military activity the text describes. The second map shows the route of the imperial army on its march towards Rome. The third map shows Rome and the points of attack by imperial forces. Following the text I have added an afterword in which I discuss some of the aspects of Renaissance warfare that are exemplified in the text. I try to highlight the institutional aspects of warfare and draw some connections with operations in the New World. My focus is very pragmatic, and I draw on the military culture Luigi describes and comments on. Consequently I neglect much of the lively Renaissance debate on peacemaking and the limitation of warfare. The afterword is followed by a brief bibliography and a glossary. Rather than include an index, I have added a resource which, I hope, makes the text more readable and supplements and refreshes the memory. I have cross-referenced liberally.

I began work on this project during a brief return visit to the American Academy in Rome in December 1990. I would like to thank the then Director, Joseph Connors, and especially Michael Putnam, the Professor in Charge at that time, for their gracious welcome. I would like also to thank David Bell, and as always Sallie Spence for their comments on the manuscript. Ronald Musto and Eileen Gardiner have buoyed me up with their enthusiasm and piloted me around historical embarrassments. I want to thank them for their help and acknowledge that despite their best efforts such errors as will inevitably be found here are my own.

This book is dedicated to my son, Raphael, in hopes that he will never experience the world it describes.

Cambridge, MA
October 12, 1992

INTRODUCTION

THE RAYS OF THE SETTING SUN of the fifth of
May lit up for the last time all the magnificence of the
Rome of the Renaissance, then the fairest and richest
city in all the world.... On the morning of the seventh
of May, Rome presented a spectacle that baffled de-
scription.... Everywhere there was the most ruthless
devastation, everywhere rapine and murder. The air re-
echoed to the wailings of women, the plaintive cries of
children, the barking of dogs, the neighing of chargers,
the clash of arms, and the crash of timber from the
burning houses. All accounts, even the Spanish, agree
that no age, no sex, no station, no nationality, neither
Spaniard nor German, neither church nor hospital was
spared. (Ludwig Von Pastor, *History of the Popes*, 9:387,
399)

What more criminal thing can be imagined than that
those who had once been pledged to the Christian religion should exert themselves to destroy Her.... (Letter
of Henry VIII to Cardinal Cibo, July 10, 1527, Lenzi, *Il
sacco di Roma del 1527*, pp. 13-14)

No subsequent political event made such a deep im-
pression as did the sack of Rome. The blow which the
papacy had suffered was so severe that its effects were
still being felt a hundred years later.... Many died in
the sack or in its aftermath, many left the city and
never returned. The artistic and literary circles, so
characteristic of the High Renaissance, were
completely destroyed. For Rome, at least, the sack was
of the gravest consequence, a scar on her history which
was long recalled in the popular and literary tradition
of the city. (Judith Hook, *The Sack of Rome*, p. 280)

It was as if some of the deepest and blindest forces in the collective *id* of Cinquecento Christendom had been let loose, and as if Christians were doing to the Church what they had wanted to do for a long time.... Four intertwined themes can be distinguished in Italian feeling: a sense of deep collective guilt; a desire for punishment; a need for the healing of the wounds inflicted by punishment; a longing for the restored order in which the individual was no longer free to seek his own destruction. (Frederick Hartt, "Power and the Individual in Mannerist Art," p. 233)

Here there is so much unhappiness about the situation in Rome that it is unbelievable; and let me say that with my own eyes I have seen when gentlemen have been speaking of it, as they are accustomed to do among themselves, some twenty-five of them weeping uncontrollably as if it had happened in their own houses. (Letter from Urbino, May 20, 1527, Marino Sanuto, *Diarii* 45:185-89)

The imperial generals have made the Emperor the absolute master of Italy,... yet the thing might have been accomplished without so much cruelty and shedding of blood.... There will be no business done at Rome for a long time and the city itself is so destroyed and ruined that until 200 years hence, it will not be Rome again. (Salazar to Gattinara, quoted in Hook, *Sack,* p. 281)

૭

HE SACK OF ROME in 1527 was an event of tragic and decisive importance. It brought the Renaissance, the greatest period in Italian history, to its sudden and catastrophic end. We are fortunate to possess many eyewitness accounts of all aspects of this extraordinary event. Only one contemporary account, however, offers an overview of the political and military situation in Italy that culminated in the sack of Rome. That account is here translated into English for the first time. It was written by Luigi Guicciardini. At the time of the events he describes, Guicciardini was the chief executive officer in the city of Florence. The government of Florence and the government of Rome were closely tied together then, because a member of the leading Florentine family, the Medici, was both the pope and the ruler of Florence. Giulio de' Medici, Pope Clement VII, served as spiritual leader of Christianity in a Europe that had not yet been formally split between Protestant and Catholic. In addition to his spiritual role, the pope was also the head of government in a territory that included most of the midsection of Italy. As a Medici, he directed the government of Florence. Because of Guicciardini's position in the Florentine government, he was well informed about the day to day government of the Papal States as well.

In addition to his direct contact with the governments most deeply involved in the events leading up to the sack, Luigi Guicciardini was closely tied to individuals who played important roles. His brother, Francesco, commanded the military forces of the pope. Other friends and correspondents of Luigi's were also directly involved in the events that led up to the sack, and Luigi must have learned a great deal from their letters and from conversations with them. His *History of the Sack of Rome*, then, is the account of an unusually well-informed contemporary who is familiar with political and military policy and history and well able to understand and interpret the events taking place around him. It is clear that much of the *History* was written while the events he describes were unfolding.

Despite its unique advantages, Luigi Guicciardini's *History of the Sack of Rome* is a forgotten book. No Italian edition of the work has been published since 1867; it has never been translated at any time into any language. Its author is just as obscure. Luigi Guicciardini is the older brother of the well-known historian and political figure, Francesco Guicciardini. Francesco's role in the political events of his time was a major one. His *History of Italy*, covering events of the years 1490 to 1534, is widely known and has often been translated. To judge from the endurance of their reputations as men of affairs and the success of their writings, there is a talented and capable Guicciardini, and another who played no meaningful part in the events of his era and left no significant record of his experiences and observations. To judge the brothers in this fashion is logical, and the comparison I have sketched out is one that is usually repeated when the elder Guicciardini is remembered at all. History's indifference to Luigi and fondness for Francesco notwithstanding, the two brothers and their achievements are not so remarkably different. As the *History of the Sack of Rome* reveals, Luigi is a capable writer and an important actor in great political and social events. Indeed, Luigi's *History* reveals an insightful and thoughtful man who tries to play a responsible part in the various crises that threatened his city and country. He assessed the larger historical situation in which he found himself intelligently, compassionately and with a clear sense of the political, social, and military consequences of the events he witnessed. Given the greater equality between the Guicciardini brothers that this text suggests, it is fitting that at a climactic moment in the *History*, the two brothers work side by side to resolve a political crisis in Florence.

LIFE OF LUIGI GUICCIARDINI

uigi Guicciardini (1478-1551) was the eldest son of Piero Guicciardini (1454-1513).[1] The Guicciardini had been an important family in Florence since the fourteenth century, and both Piero and Luigi are names that recur throughout the genealogy. The family, which still survives and still lives in the Palazzo Guicciardini, became wealthy and prominent as owners of silk factories. Their wealth quickly led them to positions of political power. The economic historian of the Renaissance, Richard Goldthwaite, notes that

> up to the very end of the republic, the Guicciardini held an extraordinary number of offices at all levels including all together forty-four priorates and sixteen tenures of the office of Gonfaloniere and several of them were knighted by the commune.[2]

Luigi Guicciardini himself seems to have had little interest in or inclination for business. His political career on the other hand was very active. He held political office first in 1514, when at the age of thirty-six he was appointed consul for the sea in the Florentine-controlled government of Pisa. In 1517 he was made commissioner of Arezzo. The following year he was elected one of the priors of Florence for the months of January and February. He served as commissioner again in 1521 and 1526, first in the small city of Castrocaro and afterwards in Pisa. In March and April of 1527, at the very height of the events he narrates in his *History*, he was appointed to the supreme executive office in Florence, that of *gonfaloniere di giustizia*. While he held that office, a political coup was attempted that would have removed the Medici from power. Luigi's role in the coup has been regarded by some as pivotal, and he has been blamed for failing to support either the rebels or the Medici. As he describes the situation in the *History*, however, it appears more accurate to say that he prevented an ill-considered and potentially disastrous coup attempt from becoming the blood-bath it threatened to be.

Although he sympathized with those opposing Medici government, Luigi's political views were by no means democratic. Goldthwaite regards him as sharing "the oligarchical sympathies of many of the city's leading patricians who were desperate to free themselves from the tightening hold of the Medici after 1512."[3]

Though he distrusted the Medici, Luigi Guicciardini, in company with all those Florentines who shared his views, found himself with no viable political alternative to them and increasingly served their interests. He was one of the consultants to Pope Clement VII on the reorganization of the Florentine government after 1530.[4] He served on the Medici-controlled Senate in 1532, and throughout the remainder of his life held numerous state offices under them. These included:

1532	Commissioner of Pisa
1534-35	Commissioner of Arezzo
1536-37	Commissioner in Florence
1537-38	Commissioner in Pistoia
1540	Commissioner in Pisa
1542-43	Commissioner of Castrocaro
1548-49	Commissioner and Captain of Arezzo

The *History of the Sack of Rome* is dedicated to Cosimo de' Medici, who assumed control of the government in Florence in 1537, and eventually became the first of the grand dukes of Tuscany. It is this familiarity with, if not always sympathy for, the Medici that gives him his unique position for observing and analyzing the events culminating in the sack of Rome in 1527. That tragedy

naturally focuses on Rome, but because Clement VII is a
member of the Medici family, his political base is Tuscan.
In his own right as *gonfaloniere* of Florence in 1527,
through the channels of information-gathering open to
the Florentine chancery, and as the correspondent of his
brother, Francesco, who is lieutenant-general of the papal
army, Luigi Guicciardini is well-situated to know the
events he narrates. Moreover, the political and military
story of the sack as he tells it has its origins in Florentine
and Medici politics as well as Roman and papal ones.

To this story, he brings literary tastes and abilities also
reflected in other works, though none of any modern
reputation. These include dialogues on political and social issues mostly focused on Florence as well as historical
narratives. Only one of them has been published in this
century. Although it has not been translated into
English, its English title would be *On Savonarola, or a
Dialogue Between Francesco Zati and Pieradovardo
Giachinotti the Day After the Battle of Gavinana*. The
other works of Luigi Guicciardini are found only in manuscript. They include works whose English titles would be:
*A Dialogue Between Baccio Valori, Giovanni Ruccelai, Paolo
Vettori, and Luigi Guicciardini on the Events of Their
Lifetimes; A Comparison of the Game of Chess with the Art
of War; A Narrative of the Ouster of Pietro de' Medici;* and
A Discourse to the Duke Alexander.

Literature was part of the Guicciardini family tradition. Luigi's father was both a successful businessman and
a humanist with interests in Greek and Latin literature
and philosophy as well as sacred studies. His reputation
for study brought him to the attention of Marsiglio
Ficino (1433-99), one of the most prominent scholars of
the Renaissance.[5] Piero's humanism may have formed the
foundation for the flowering of literary interest and
productivity in succeeding generations of the Guicciardini family.

Luigi also played a role in the writings of others, primarily those of his brother, Francesco. Francesco and Luigi corresponded through most of their lives, and many of the younger Guicciardini's letters, the majority of which have been published, concern or are addressed to Luigi. The Florentine political and social analyst, Niccolò Machiavelli, shared many interests and opinions with Luigi. A few letters from Machiavelli to Luigi survive, and among them is one of Machiavelli's most famous and most bizarre. Luigi is the recipient of the notorious letter of December 8, 1509, in which Machiavelli describes a real or imagined encounter with a superannuated prostitute in Verona. Machiavelli also dedicated one of the sections of his long poem *Capitoli* or "Chapters" to Luigi. The section is entitled "On Ambition."[6] Luigi's interest in the arts was not entirely confined to literature. He befriended the Renaissance painter and art historian, Giorgio Vasari. Vasari painted a portrait of Luigi that does not survive, but he also included a representation of him in a fresco in the Palazzo Vecchio, painted in 1559, that can still be seen today.

LUIGI GUICCIARDINI AS A HISTORIAN

 uigi's interest in writing history grew out of his political activity. He shared the Florentine belief that history writing was "a primary vehicle for expressing political commitment."[7] Mark Phillips has explored the manifestations of that attitude in both well known and little known Florentine works; he concludes:

> At its deepest level, history writing was an act of citizenship, the expression of pragmatic commitments to the public world. In the absence of a body of formal political theory, historiography served as the major literature of political commentary.[8]

We should not look to Luigi, then, for a passive representation of the great events of his period. His aim in recording those events was indeed to offer "political commentary." The events surrounding the sack of Rome were dramatic and their effects were devastating. Luigi saw them as extreme and exemplary cases of the issues with which contemporary political leaders had to come to terms. At every step in his story, he offered his opinion as an experienced and thoughtful politician on the wisdom or imprudence of decisions made and actions carried out. Rather than seeing him in the historian's mold as an objective recorder of facts, it might be helpful if we imagined him as a Renaissance proponent of the "case study" method.

Like his friend Machiavelli, Luigi viewed history more or less the way a political scientist or sociologist might view it today. He focused on governments and what they were trying to achieve, but he was equally conscious of the means with which they worked to reach their goals. In setting general policy directions he looked for plans that were neither too ambitious nor too conservative, properly timed and appropriate to the situation at hand. The primary material governments have to work with are people. The social groups Luigi took into account were leaders, citizens, and soldiers. Luigi judged political leaders on their ability to provide a safe and productive social environment in which citizens enjoyed the maximum liberty for individual achievement. Rulers were also judged on their ability to set rational goals for their societies. Military leaders were judged for their ability to wage war prudently and successfully. A commander who avoided all risks and one who took too many risks were both condemned.

To this essential rationality of means and ends and a commitment to preserving the liberties of citizens, Luigi added some notions about the best form of life for men and women. To his way of thinking, the good life is one that makes a society stable and long-lasting. Such viability is guaranteed by two things, moderation and military discipline. By moderation Luigi meant the limitation of economic and sexual excess. By military discipline he meant something like the Roman Republican ideal of lifetime training and readiness for military service. While it is easy to see the avoidance of economic and sexual excess as primary Christian values, Luigi regards both of his prime virtues as consistent with Christianity. His social theory is a fusion of classical values and early Christian virtues. The classicism is something he shares with most cultured men and women of the Renaissance. His particular brand of Christianity, with its austerity suggesting the emerging Protestant and Catholic Reformations more strongly than contemporary Catholicism, is derived from the Florentine reformer-priest Savonarola. His views are thus generically Renaissance and particularly Florentine.

Like many other Renaissance thinkers, Guicciardini viewed history as cyclical and repetitive. The forces that move history and bend it towards cyclical repetition, he thought, were to be found in the interplay between human nature and customs on the one hand and political styles on the other. The cycles he observes are movements along the scale of good and evil Fortune. Luigi Guicciardini introduces us to this idea in the Dedicatory Letter fronting his *History*. In what seems at first to be just an elaborate apology for his choice of subject matter, Luigi describes how a taste for history was developed in the ancient world. Greece and Rome are his frequent standards for what is normal or superior in human activity, as it is for most thinkers of the Renaissance. As his letter unfolds, however, history writing in the ancient world is characterized as a response to the first great downward trend in human history, identified by the classical myth of the Golden Age. This was a time when humanity lived in peace and harmony together; there was no wickedness, no inequality, no greed, and no scarcity. Gradually, however, wickedness – either represented or invented by particular human beings – took the place of the universal contentment that marked the first era. As wickedness increased, human fortunes declined. In the era of lowest ebb, unnamed in the mythical past but compared with the Italy of Guicciardini's own day, human affairs reached their lowest point. In those times, the ancient historians used all their ingenuity to call to mind and to represent pleasing and inspiring events from the past to provide recreation and relief to their readers.

In a sense Luigi Guicciardini identified classical history writing with nostalgia, maybe even nostalgia for the Golden Age. In this mythical account of the origins of history, however, he is also showing us one half of the fundamental pattern of human history and the one most significant for his own era, that of decline. Guicciardini confirms the mythical pattern of history-writing by writing in a period of decline, but he contradicts his mythical model when he proposes to write what he calls a tragedy rather than the conventional nostalgic history of past successes. He had no wish to dwell on horrors or misery for their own sake, but he wanted to take advantage of the unique opportunity that low points offer. In his cyclical view, Guicciardini regarded extreme lows as turning points. When things are as bad as they can get, there is nowhere to go but up, and Luigi hoped to show how the negative example of Italy's disaster could point the way towards future success. The history of the sack teaches what to avoid in social, political, military, and diplomatic affairs. Luigi aimed to press those lessons home and argue from them for a series of positive reforms that would, he hoped, be the beginning of Italy's return to greatness.

Despite his hopes, no such return to greatness began in the sixteenth century. Italy's fortunes did not significantly improve until the nineteenth century, and even then she did not occupy a place on the European stage that matched the greatness of the Roman Empire. None-theless the lessons Guicciardini drew from the sack were prophetic of trends in other nations that did rise to prominence on the world stage during the sixteenth cen-tury. The ideals he espoused were an amalgam of Roman Republican and Apostolic Christian virtues. Among his most fundamental political beliefs are these ideals:

1. While stupid princes are an unmitigated disaster, the best government is that of a single wise and prudent individual who is advised by a small and select counsel of men. The best advisers are those who have made a practice of observing the patterns of human affairs. Larger groups of advisers or deliberative assemblies are prone to faction-alism and unreasonable preferences, and they cannot be trusted.

2. A citizen militia is the key both to military security and to the cultivation of those virtues that make a state successful and long-lasting.

3. Frugality, moderation, and self-discipline are the principal virtues of successful and enduring states.

4. Self-indulgence, greed, and the unlimited pursuit of pleasure, especially the many varieties of sexual grati-fication, are the forces that destroy societies most quickly. Greed, stinginess, and lust are the major problems of cities and states governed by clerics. Church government, consequently, is among the worst forms, in his view.

5. Luigi prefers activist military commanders who combine prudence with courage. To his mind a great commander is identified by the ability to seize opportuni-ties when they present themselves. His strategic thinking is weak, and his notion of tactics is reactive, since the emphasis was on seizing rather than creating opportuni-ties. The great military leaders in his story possess traits that distance them but do not distinguish them from Luigi's brother, Francesco. As the lieutenant-general of papal forces, Francesco Guicciardini fought a defensive war that prevented a direct attack on Florence. Bad com-

manders, however, are timid and vacillating. They, too, rely on defense; they seldom take the offensive, and if they do, they can achieve victory only with overwhelming force.

6. Political leaders are not very different from military ones. The good ones tend to be decisive, the bad ones vacillate. Ironically, good political leaders and strong military commanders have a tendency to impose their will unfairly and to suppress the liberties of those who are in their power.

THE EVENTS LEADING UP TO THE SACK

 he *History of the Sack of Rome* describes events that occurred between May 22, 1526 and early summer 1527. The beginning point is the date of the publication of a treaty that established what became known as the Holy League or the League of Cognac. The treaty was signed in the French city of Cognac by representatives from England, France, Florence, Venice, Milan, and the Papacy. The end point of the *History* is much less precise. It comes after the city of Rome had been invaded and sacked and while it was still occupied by enemy troops. Thus the *History of the Sack of Rome* is the history of a military alliance of two nations, England and France, and three Italian city-states. This military alliance was formed in opposition to the empire of Charles V, who ruled Spain, the Netherlands, and most of Germany. Charles also ruled substantial parts of Italy at this time, and these Italian possessions and the emperor's intentions of increasing his power over Italy were what the pope and the Italian city-states were most concerned about. England and France joined the alliance for different reasons. England joined to help maintain a balance of power in Europe which Henry VIII and his chief advisor, Cardinal Wolsey, thought was threatened by the emperor at this point. France joined the Holy League for less abstract motives. In a recent war between France and the emperor, which was fought primarily over the issue of the control of territories in Italy, not only had France been defeated, but the French king, Francis I, had been captured. To end his long captivity, Francis I was obliged to sign a very disadvantageous treaty with the emperor. By its terms he lost Burgundy, and to ensure its observation, he was obliged to hand over two of his sons as hostages to Charles V. He repudiated that treaty almost the moment he was released; and France joined the Holy League to recover what it had just lost in the preceding war.

To understand the war in which France lost so much and the emperor made such great gains, it is necessary momentarily to step still further back in time and look at events in Europe and Italy beginning in 1494. If we do this, two large patterns of events are apparent. One of these is the consolidation and organization within boundaries still recognizable today of France, Spain, and England. This consolidation enabled those nations to play a role in European and world politics that required a financial and demographic base larger than that possessed by any political entity of the Middle Ages. In the case of Spain, this consolidation reached beyond national borders, since Spain after 1519 was governed by an emperor with hereditary claim to many other territories in Europe and in the New World. This consolidation of territories under one government at the national level or beyond is dramatically countered by Italy. Despite the dream of a united Italy that had been shared by many since the days of Dante, the Italian peninsula remained fragmented during the Renaissance. The little states that made it up were in constant flux, and boundaries shifted repeatedly as wars and alliances changed the political scene. These tiny states at odds with each other sometimes entered alliances with the larger nations in hopes of besting a local adversary. Sometimes the political confusion of the peninsula offered opportunities for conquest that stronger neighboring nations did not resist.

The fundamental imbalance between large national or supranational states on the one hand and tiny city states on the other transformed Italy into a battleground. On this battleground the local states still played important roles, but the short life of gains and losses in victory and defeat and the constant openness of the peninsula to invasion reflected the absence of definitive power within Italy.

Peter Partner in his excellent history of Renaissance Rome has summed the situation up in these terms:

> The French invasion of Italy in 1494 began the long agony of the Italian states, both the city-states and the feudal kingdom of Naples. By the opening of the second decade of the sixteenth century the role of the Italian powers had been transformed. Milan, Florence and the Neapolitan kingdom had become the instruments of the European policies of the great powers.[9]

Italy in this period was like the Lebanon of the 1970s and 1980s, or like the New World before the European colonies won their independence. It was a place where European powers fought battles, often with local allies, that were staged very far away from where their causes originated. Italian conquest was of interest to these contending forces, but their opposition was not confined to this single issue, and much of the fighting in Italy would have made more sense if it had occurred somewhere else. What is truly extraordinary is that Renaissance art, architecture, and literature could have reached their high point in exactly the period when Italy was suffering repeated foreign invasion.

The War of the League of Cognac, then, is only one of many wars that raged in the first third of the sixteenth century. But its decisive ending in the sack of Rome marks it off from the others and gives it greater significance. As a way of approaching it, however, and introducing the men who played the greatest political and military roles in it, I will describe in some detail the war that preceded it and determined many of its major features.

The war, which ended so disastrously for the French when their king was captured and large numbers of their nobles were killed, itself began as a rebound from attack. imperial forces had twice driven a French army from Italy in a period of two years. The French retreated after their loss at La Bicocca, in northern Italy on April 27, 1522. They invaded again and were routed by imperial troops at Sesia near Milan almost exactly two years later on April 30, 1524. The poor showing against imperial troops that these campaigns reflected encouraged Emperor Charles V and King Henry VIII of England to plan a three-pronged invasion of France. Charles was to invade from Spain, Henry from the north. The third prong of the attack, and the only one that ever came into being, was to be led by two imperial commanders from the direction of Italy. These men were Fernando de Avalos, more commonly known as the marquis of Pescara, and Charles de Bourbon. Pescara came from a noble Spanish family, but he had lived all his life in Italy; he had long been a general in the imperial army. This would be his last military campaign. Charles de Bourbon, the other imperial commander in this campaign, was a newcomer to the imperial ranks. Until 1523 he had served his cousin, Francis I, as a high-ranking prince and important military leader. He was named *connetable,* or constable, of the kingdom of France in 1515. His popularity and vast territorial holdings, however, made him a dangerous rival to the king, who was eager to establish complete control over all French territory. Francis' method for disposing of his dangerous subordinate was a law-suit brought by the queen-mother. Bourbon's response was to rebel against the king and take service with Charles V.

Because of his huge domains in France and his personal popularity, Bourbon believed that he could be the focus of a French uprising against Francis 1. In company with the other imperial commanders, he judged the French to be militarily inferior. On June 30, 1524 (two months after the French defeat at Sesia) an imperial army led by Bourbon and Pescara began an invasion of southern France from the direction of Italy. By August 15, 1524, after a series of surrenders and easy victories throughout Provence, they had laid siege to the city of Marseilles. Here their invasion reached its sudden conclusion. The resistance put up by the town was unexpectedly strong. In anticipation of the attack, the walls of Marseilles had been reinforced by an Italian specialist in military architecture named Renzo da Ceri. (In 1527 he was to lead the defenders of Rome against Bourbon's troops with entirely opposite results.) During its month-long siege of Marseilles the imperial army was supported by Genoese ships led by the greatest admiral of the sixteenth century, Andrea Doria. In the War of the League of Cognac, Doria's superiority at sea was to be one of the few bright points in the League's campaigning. With all its strength and tactical support, the imperial army had to admit defeat, and on September 29, 1524 Bourbon and Pescara gave up their attempt to take Marseilles and abandoned the invasion of France. They began to retreat along the French Riviera towards Genoa.

The king of France in person then led his army on yet another invasion of Italy. Rather than pursuing the retreating enemy, he made directly for Italy through the Argentière Pass in the Alps. The invasion had the combined goal of recapturing territory lost in the preceding defeats and destroying the imperial army. Its immediate goal was be to reach Milan before the imperial army, worn out by the siege of Marseilles and taking the longer coastal route. In this, Francis and his army were successful. On October 24, 1524, while the imperial forces were still en route, the advance guard of the French army reached Milan. The city and the Lombardy region surrounding it were ruled by Duke Francesco Maria Sforza. While his family and that of the Visconti, whom the Sforzas succeeded, had held power in Lombardy since the late thirteenth century, Francesco Sforza himself had only recently come to power. In 1521, when the imperial forces ousted the French, they placed Sforza on the throne. When the French returned, the duke fled the city and joined his troops to the still weak imperial forces in Italy.

The French arrival in Milan and the success of their plan to outrun the imperial army turned out to be something of an anti-climax. In the late summer of 1524, Milan experienced a very severe outbreak of plague. For this reason the imperial army had abandoned the city, leaving only the central fortress, or Castello, of Milan defended by a contingent of troops. The rest of the city surrendered to the marquis of Saluzzo. At that time the marquis commanded the vanguard, or fast moving shock-troops, which preceded the main body of the French army. In the War of the League of Cognac, the marquis of Saluzzo was to lead the small French army which eventually arrived in Italy to aid its allies in the Holy League. Just as the duke and the imperial forces had abandoned the plague-infested City, so did the French troops. In fact, their motivation was two-fold. Not only were they avoiding the plague, but they were searching for the imperial army. That army, led by the viceroy of Naples, Lannoy, at first had headed towards the nearby city of Pavia. Rather than risk battle with the superior French force, the imperial army had left Pavia almost as soon as it arrived. The bulk of the imperial forces had retreated toward the small cities of Lodi and Crema southeast of Milan. A small imperial garrison was left in Pavia under the direction of Antonio de Leva. The entire army of France commanded by its king was now facing that small garrison.

Such an overwhelming military advantage should have led to the immediate capture of Pavia. Antonio de Leva, however, was a very resourceful commander in this war as in the war to follow. His small contingent of troops kept the French army at bay. By mid-December, the French had gotten nowhere in their invasion. They had control of Milan, but the plague there made it too dangerous to remain in the city. They were besieging Pavia, but they seemed unable to capture it. Worst of all they were doing no damage to the imperial army that they had come to Italy to destroy.

At this point in the war, the political situation in Italy was beginning to change. Pope Clement, who had been strongly favorable to the emperor until this time, began to feel that it might be advisable to support the French in order to counterbalance imperial gains in the peninsula. Such shifts occurred repeatedly in Italian politics, as the small states there sought to maintain their freedom of action by getting the major powers to neutralize each other. Pope Clement opened secret negotiations with the French, urging them to attempt the reconquest of Naples. Francis, who was achieving nothing in the north of Italy, detached a third of his army – about fifteen thousand men – and sent them south to invade the kingdom of Naples. The political climate in Italy favored this invasion; the military situation, too, was favorable, since the majority of the imperial army remained in the north on the alert against the invading French. The season was unfavorable though. Bad weather slowed down the army, and food and fuel were scarce. The planned invasion of southern Italy came to nothing; but the detachment of one-third of his force left King Francis very vulnerable to imperial counter-attack. In the War of the League of Cognac the two footholds of the imperial forces in Italy – Milan in the north and Naples in the south – were to present similar opportunities and similar pitfalls. Success in one region could always be countered or even checkmated by decisive action in the other. The forces united against the Empire were always threatened by a two-front war.

While Francis was besieging Pavia, the imperial army had time to regroup itself. Although Venice was allied with the Empire in this war, the change in papal policy that I have already described affected the Venetians, too. They failed to supply their allies with the troops that had been pledged. Consequently, Bourbon went in search of mercenary troops in one of the two customary places. Swiss mercenaries had long been hired to fight in Italy; and the Swiss guards who police the Vatican today in their Renaissance uniforms are modern representatives of this age-old practice.

Bourbon, however, sought his troops in another region, from which troops reputedly superior to the Swiss had recently begun to be recruited. These were German soldiers known as *Landsknechts,* or lancers. They were to play a crucial role in the War of the League of Cognac, and especially in the sack of Rome. This was due not only to their military ability, but also to the fact that among them were many followers of the German religious reformer, Martin Luther. While as yet there was no formal split between Catholics and Lutherans, these men, and their leader, George von Frundsberg, were militantly antipapal. Their religious ideals had no part to play in a war against France, but of course in 1527 they would prove important.

With these new recruits, the imperial army reached a size that made it capable of attacking the French, especially since the French army had been shrunk by the detachment of a third of its strength. The imperial forces assembled in Lodi, then moved to a point on the road between Pavia and Milan, hoping to provoke the French to abandon Pavia in order to protect the larger and more important Lombard city. The French did not take the bait, and the imperial army, which had no intention of occupying Milan, moved toward Pavia. They attacked and overwhelmed a strong-point on the road that had been designed to protect the French against counter-attack, and continued moving towards Pavia. The French took up new positions in preparation for the assault. Francis and the bulk of his army moved towards the east of the city; they left behind a small force of Swiss mercenaries and Italian troops known as the "Black Bands." These troops were led by a Florentine with a dramatic role to play in the War of the League of Cognac. He is Giovanni de' Medici, often called Giovanni delle Bande Nere (of the Black Bands) because of his leadership of these crack troops. They had just disavowed their allegiance to the imperial army and the duke of Milan, Francesco Maria Sforza, by whom they had been employed.

Giovanni de' Medici was born in Florence in 1498. As a military leader, he was noted for his personal courage, and especially for two characteristics that were uncommon among military men in the Renaissance. Unlike most of his contemporaries, he preferred infantry and light horsemen to heavy cavalry. He was also one of the very first commanders to take personal responsibility for the welfare of his troops. This highly skilled and highly motivated group of about two thousand men took the name "Le Bande Nere" from black stripes on their armor that they first wore in mourning for the death of Pope Leo X. Giovanni delle Bande Nere and his skilled troops were the one consistent bright spot in the military command of the League of Cognac.

As his family name indicates, Giovanni belonged to the Medici dynasty that governed Florence. His defection from the imperial army probably reflected the change in allegiance of Pope Clement VII. Giovanni descended from the junior or cadet branch of the family, however, and that branch had never held power in Florence while the senior branch continued to produce male heirs. Nevertheless, because of his temperament and his administrative ability, Giovanni was feared not only by citizens of Florence, like Luigi Guicciardini, who hoped to escape from the tyranny of Medici government, but by members of the senior branch of the Medici family itself. Pope Clement VII, who led the senior branch of the family at this point, seemed always to have a war for Giovanni to take part in. Many historians believe that his intention was not just to take advantage of the finest Italian military leader of the period, but also to expose the potential usurper to the continual risk of death. If so, his policy nearly succeeded at Pavia. On February 17, 1525, while skirmishing with troops from the besieged town, Giovanni delle Bande Nere was struck by a sniper's bullet that shattered his foot. With a safe-conduct provided by the marquis of Pescara, he was taken to the nearby town of Piacenza to be treated. That he did not lose his life, or at least his leg, is a tribute to his good fortune, not to the medical science of the period. With their leader disabled, the Black Bands vanished from the war.

It is events of this kind that distinguish the warfare of the Renaissance most markedly from modern warfare. No national identity or other deep commitment tied Giovanni and his troops to the imperial cause, and they did not hesitate to change sides, even at such a crucial point in the war. No one thought of what they had done as treachery. Indeed, when Giovanni was wounded, Pescara, his former commander and now his nominal enemy, granted him safe-conduct through enemy lines so that his wounds could be treated. With their leader absent, his troops disappeared. Their loyalty was not to a cause but to their condottiere. That familiar word suggests not only military leader, but also something like the modern word "contractor." Without him, the army – the specialized labor-force he has engaged to supply – has no connection to the troops they have been fighting beside.

At about the same time that Giovanni was wounded and his men dispersed, six thousand additional troops left the French army to resist attacks on their home territory. These were men of the northern Italian region of Grisone, which had been attacked by soldiers of the duke of Milan, Francesco Maria Sforza. Reports of the diminution of the French army convinced the imperial commanders, Pescara, Bourbon and Lannoy, to launch an attack. Their decision was reinforced by the fact that their own troops, who had not been paid for some time, were mutinous. As was so often the case in the Renaissance, these men realized that if they wanted to keep their army, they needed to use it quickly. So on the night of February 24-25, 1525 they launched a flanking attack against the French army.

At the front of the army were engineers with explosives, picks, and shovels, supported by heavy artillery, who would be responsible for breaking through the walls of a large estate that sheltered the French. Immediately behind these men came the first contingent of troops led by the marquis of Vasto. This imperial officer was destined to succeed his uncle, the marquis of Pescara, as commander of imperial forces in Italy during the War of the League of Cognac. Following Vasto came forces led by Pescara, the Viceroy Lannoy, and finally the newly recruited German troops under Bourbon. While this army attacked from the north, Antonio de Leva led his contingent of imperial troops out of the besieged city of Pavia to attack from the opposite direction.

Despite a heroic and devastating countercharge by the French heavy cavalry with King Francis in the lead, the French army was surprised, outsmarted, and virtually destroyed. The number of men killed, especially nobles who had led the French army for many years, was staggering. The king himself was captured. As the great historian of Renaissance warfare, Charles Oman, has written:

> This was the last regular pitched battle that was fought in Italy for many a year, and we may add that it was the last general action since Marignano in which both sides were ready to take the offensive.[10]

Out of this decisive imperial victory the motive force for the League of Cognac was born. The French loss set the seal on the new anti-imperial policy of the pope and the majority of Italian states. As the imperial faction had grown steadily stronger in Italy, the Italian states had progressively deserted it. Venice failed to send the troops it had pledged to the imperial army. Probably at Clement's instigation, the troops of Giovanni delle Bande Nere changed sides and supported the French against the Empire. Far from ending warfare in the peninsula, this decisive victory convinced everyone that the only hope for Italian, French, and to a lesser degree English independence lay in opposition to the emperor. Ironically, imperial victory prompted the emperor's allies to desert him and to unite with his defeated enemy in the League of Cognac. The other progeny of Pavia is perhaps less strange. As Oman notes, Pavia convinced officers on both sides that a war of tactical advantage and avoidance of battle was much less hazardous than a winner-take-all confrontation. The warfare of the League of Cognac, we will see, reflected that lesson very well.

The last beam added to the substructure of the League of Cognac comes from another imperial ally. Francesco Maria Sforza, the duke of Milan, was prompted by the victory at Pavia to resist the power of the very emperor who had placed him on the throne. His plan was not open warfare but a clandestine operation. He sent his minister, Giovanni Morone, to the marquis of Pescara, who, despite his continual service to the Empire had received no substantial reward. Morone promised Pescara that he would be made viceroy of Naples if he abandoned the service of the emperor. Whether Pescara ever wavered or not is unclear. What is clear is that he eventually informed the emperor of the attempts made to win his allegiance. Morone was arrested and put to death. Francesco Maria Sforza, duke of Milan, was accused of treason to his overlord, the emperor, and his title was stripped from him. Imperial troops, who had been supporting his leadership in Milan, now were sent against him.

The duke and several hundred followers and soldiers took refuge in the great Castello of Milan. The Milanese people revolted against the imperial troops but were eventually subdued and subjected to harsh occupation. Francesco Maria Sforza became an adherent of the League of Cognac and his restoration to his duchy became one of its goals. Relief of the Castello of Milan became a primary military goal of the League, and much of the first book of Luigi Guicciardini's history focuses on the campaign to relieve the Castello and the city of Milan. Shortly after the Morone affair, the marquis of Pescara died. He left his nephew, the marquis of Vasto, and Antonio de Leva as his successors to the command of imperial forces in the north of Italy. His wife, the poet Vittoria Colonna, devoted much of the rest of her life to poems in praise of her late husband.

As the *History of the Sack of Rome* opens, after the Dedicatory Letter that I have already discussed, the time is late May 1526. Francis 1 is safely back in his kingdom, after months of captivity first in Italy, then in Madrid. The former enemies of the French – Venice, Florence, the Papal States, England, and the deposed Duke of Milan – have entered into an alliance against the emperor and his army in Italy. Their first goal is to aid the recently deposed duke of Milan, Francesco Maria Sforza, who has taken shelter in the Castello of Milan where he is surrounded by imperial troops. These troops are soon augmented by additional forces sent by Charles V from

Spain. They are led by Charles de Bourbon, whom the emperor named duke of Milan to replace the treacherous Sforza.

The papal forces, the Florentine forces, and the troops from Venice must first combine, and then, when their strength is sufficient, prepare to move against the imperial army that occupies Milan and a few other cities in Lombardy. Most of Book I is concerned with attacks and counterattacks in northern Italy. Perhaps the most significant event is the arrival of German troops, Lutherans for the most part, led by George von Frundsberg. They have been sent from the frontier of Austria to join with the imperial forces occupying Milan. A surprise attack on Rome, which has been left defenseless, causes the pope to accept a truce on disadvantageous terms. The truce brings the fighting in the North to a virtual end. The imperial troops in Milan finally join up with the Germans and under the leadership of Charles de Bourbon, these forces begin a long march that will lead them eventually to Rome. The League's army assumes defensive positions in response. One wing protects Florence; the other Venice. Circling wide around Florence and outdistancing his enemies, Bourbon begins an all-out march towards Rome.

Early in Book II, that march reaches its goal, and Bourbon and his army attack and easily capture Rome. Their behavior once inside the city they have captured is the subject of most of the second book.

℃

NOTES

1. Bono Simonetta, ed., *Del Savonarola. ovvero dialogo...* (Florence: Olschki, 1959); Rudolf von Albertini, *Das florentinische Staatsbewusstein im Ubergang von der Republik zum Prinzipat* (Berne: Francke, 1955).

2. Richard A. Goldthwaite, *Private Wealth in Renaissance Florence: A Study of Four Families* (Princeton: Princeton University Press, 1968), p. III.

3. Goldthwaite, *Private Wealth*, p. 133.

4. See *Archivio Storico Italiano* I (1842): 420-67, for the eight *pareri* (assessments) including Luigi's, solicited by Clement VII on the form Medici government should take.

5. Goldthwaite, *Private Wealth*, p. 130; Paul Oscar Kristeller, *Studies in Renaissance Thought and Letters* (Rome: Ed. di storia e letteratura, 1956), p. 444; idem, *Supplementum Ficinianum* (Florence: Olschki, 1937), 2:344.

6. Giorgio Inglese, ed., *Niccolò Machiavelli Capitoli* (Rome: Bulzoni, 1981), p. 143.

7. Mark Phillips, *The Memoir of Marco Parenti* (Princeton: Princeton University Press, 1987), p. vii.

8. Ibid.

9. Peter Partner, *Renaissance Rome 1500-1550* (Berkeley, Los Angeles, London: University of California Press, 1976), p. 25.

10. Charles Oman, *A History of the Art of War in the Sixteenth Century* (London: Methuen, 1937), p. 205.

* *
*

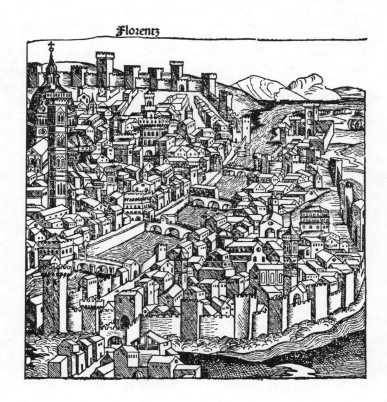
Florentz

DEDICATION

TO THE MOST ILLUSTRIOUS AND MOST
EXCELLENT LORD,
LORD COSIMO DE' MEDICI, SECOND DUKE OF
THE FLORENTINE REPUBLIC,
LUIGI GUICCIARDINI'S GREETING.

 OST ILLUSTRIOUS DUKE: When ancient historians wanted to commit some event of their time to literary memory, they racked their brains to find either the most interesting or the most glorious event that had occurred with which to satisfy the taste of their readers. To assure their own fame, they ornamented their histories with whatever eloquence nature and art had conceded them. Now voluntary poverty and natural justice – two basic and true virtues that had kept men happy and secure in the time of Janus during the Golden Age – had long since abandoned human minds; and, because of the arrogance and ferocity of Ninus king of the Assyrians, the first disturber of human peace (if we are to believe the Greek historians), ambition and the desire for domination had taken their place in the human heart. From these vices came hatred, warfare, cruelty, and avarice, along with every other wicked and vile perversion. And little by little these vices brought so many terrible forms of life into being that miserable mortals often came to feel and know the arrogance of Briareus, the cruelty of Phalaris, the greed of Midas, and the lust of Sardanapolis by experience. Through such monstrous transformations of princes and peoples, human life finally reached its lowest ebb (as at present), and men and

I

women experienced nothing but trials and infinite, pressing miseries.

Under these conditions it wasn't surprising (since the human race was tasting and sampling more bitterness than sweetness every day), that, in order to cheer themselves up and lighten their hearts after the torments they had borne, readers preferred books that were enjoyable over others that only added unhappiness to unhappiness. And if this desire were naturally to be found in everyone's heart in the past, it is no less certain to be found there at present. For from the time of the invasion of King Charles VIII of France until the very recent destruction of Rome, there have been continual and brutal wars, unheard-of famine, and unusually severe outbreaks of plague in this unhappy Italy. To these disasters the violent deaths of innumerable multitudes of people, government overthrows, and insatiable plundering must be added.

These many and various scourges have caused irreparable damage to the principal cities and ruined all the princes who were strong and secure before the invasion of the French king. Indeed not only has Italy obviously been brought to a low ebb by so many disasters, but most of the rest of Europe is a partner in our ruin. In like manner (since it is the nature of evil, like fire in flammable material, to spread if it is not quickly put out), Europe, too, might in a short time be brought to its final extermination. Only some new legislator or new monarch (like those who have arisen in past centuries in similar disasters) might have the power and sense of justice to restrain and chase back to hell the unbridled and diabolical Furies that have in recent years swept violently through every land. Through his goodness and virtue, such a man could return human life to that state that was ordained for it in the primal era by innocent Nature.

Most Illustrious and Excellent Duke, during these great and miserable calamities of ours, I considered how good it would be to follow the practices of those wise writers of the past and only describe things that refresh the heart of the reader. (This would mean ignoring topics that terrify the reader as much as they terrify those who experienced them). But when I found myself incapable of imitating the Ancients in this regard, I was reluctant to publish under your most fortunate name the most lugubrious, the most frightening, and the most shameful tragedy that Omnipotent Wisdom has yet put on in this unfortunate Italian, and indeed, nearly worldwide stage. As I wrote during those terrible days, it was not my intention to derive pleasure from revisiting with the pen the scene of so many and such pitiable cruelties. I wanted instead to keep continually before my eyes a strong example of the great evils that arrogance and immoderate ambition cause and of the need for erring men to anticipate and to fear divine justice.

Indeed, whoever diligently considers the source of the continual variation in the fortunes of republics and kingdoms can learn from the illustrious example of Rome the causes that have brought cities and empires little by little to prominence, and then, as they decline from this eminence, those that lead to their ultimate evil and ruin. In fact, despite these seemingly opposite motions up and down, human undertakings tend to oscillate between one extreme and the other; and ultimately nothing changes but names and places. Bearing this in mind, anyone who considers this miraculous earthly round of close to seven thousand years' duration (according to sacred histories) with acute and pious sight would have to confess that man's perfection cannot be attained in this miserable and brief terrestrial life, but only in that otherworldly one that is eternal and most blessed.   ·

Most Illustrious Duke, I delayed publishing my history for one further reason, namely because in this account the bitter and catastrophic death of your illustrious and warlike father is described. My aim was to delight you with my writing, not give you reason to be unhappy. At last, though, I realized that death (common to everyone in every era) should not cause the living to mourn for those who have passed gloriously to the other life, as Your Excellency's most illustrious father plainly did. His death was the turning point of the war, occurring at the very moment when, because of his brave actions, he was most appreciated by his colleagues and most feared by his enemies. When the hope he had inspired in our army and the fear he had inspired in the enemy were at their peak, leaving behind immortal fame, he was carried away to heaven. Clearly the Divine Majesty intended that Rome should be prey to the imperial army, and so it was essential that the army of the League should be deprived of his excellent virtues – and not by human but by diabolical force. Then without any obstacles, after overrunning the whole of Italy, the imperial army could reach the city of Rome.

From this account, Your Excellency will understand how much God favors the worthy and humane undertakings of the emperor; and little by little discloses that He has designated him monarch of the universe, fit with his rare goodness and unique prudence to reorganize the ruined world. This is material that should certainly refresh and gladden your noble heart, and spur it to be worthy of such a glorious father and of the loyalty that you justly owe to the grandeur of the imperial majesty. Indeed by many and many a sign it is clear to anyone who tallies up your virtuous achievements and youthful years, that your valor will surpass your father's just as up till now your good fortune has surpassed his. I hope one day to demonstrate this in a work free from adulation.

If, however, Your Excellency should judge that this terrible tragedy, confined and divided into two books, has not been narrated by me with that order, elegance, or artfulness that a true literary achievement would require; that is because I have not made a career of eloquence, or studied the rules that enable others to write their celebrated and delightful works. I write in those simple and common words that are natural for me, presenting the naked truth that such an exemplary story requires. Indeed it would have been easier for me to leave out many details of its miseries and cruelties (since every day from that unlucky city one hears of new torments and new victims) than to make things up so that it would seem more savage and horrible, as the ancient poets and orators did in their imaginary tragedies.

And so, having placed it in the protecting shadow of your most brilliant name, may it not prove tedious or unpleasant to Your Excellency (when you are less occupied with the very grave concerns of the Republic) to consider and examine it with diligence. I am convinced that if it can satisfy Your Excellency it can readily defend itself from anyone who might accuse me of presumption. I have noted the errors of various men and given everyone the credit he deserved: whoever writes history should do it honestly. Part of the historian's task is to teach the advisers of republics and princes how to live by using the true examples of others. His greater role is to encourage the great men of the future to imitate the noblest virtues and the best customs of celebrated men and to shun the negative qualities of those who have counseled or acted unwisely in service of their countries.

And should Your Excellency judge of it otherwise, throw it in the fire: if it fails to please your wide-ranging intellect, it neither could nor should please another's.

But to what purpose am I straining to increase the length of this letter with such ceremonious and superfluous words, knowing them very well to be the enemies of truth? Therefore here follows the introduction and the narration of our most true tragedy promised and dedicated to Your Excellency.

ↁ

BOOK ONE

PROLOGUE

N THE VERY RECENT PAST, in the noblest and richest city of Europe, the least
resisted, most thorough, and most accursed
pillage – the like of which was never seen
in past centuries – was carried out by the
most savage and impious nations to be found in our time.
I set myself to write about it, to the extent that my weak
intellect could encompass it. This unique and terrible
event makes clear how serious and harmful a mistake it is
to underestimate an enemy, or for a disunited population, unaccustomed to arms and without military leaders,
nourished at leisure on lascivious delights, to persuade
itself that it can resist stubborn, hardened, and hungry
troops. That is a completely mistaken notion and the
main reason that the ancient and beautiful city of Rome
experienced a humiliation beyond that which any other
city ever endured.

For indeed, while the proud and ambitious city of
Carthage was captured and destroyed by the younger
Scipio with greater violence and with more cruelty, her
citizens were neither ignorant nor indifferent. And even
though the populous and heavily fortified city of
Jerusalem was depopulated and burned by the emperors
Vespasian and Titus, nonetheless, through a thousand
trials and dangers during their four-year siege, the
Romans gained great respect for the strength and tenac-
ity of the Jews. In the time of our fathers the effeminate
and disunited city of Constantinople was subjugated by

Muhammed, king of the Turks, and the dominion and authority of the last Greek emperor, Constantine, who then ruled the Eastern Empire, were altogether extinguished. He and his men were not killed, however, in so few hours nor by so small a number of enemy troops. Five years ago the invincible island of Rhodes was attacked and taken by force by Sultan Suleiman, grandson of the aforementioned Muhammed. Not in a short time, though, nor without sustaining very heavy casualties, did he at last (but only through a treaty) become its sovereign. Finally, Rome itself, pillaged and burned by barbarians so many other times, was never before captured and sacked with such ease, nor in such brief time, nor by so few forces.

Anyone who considers the capture of these other famous cities, and how they fell into the hands of their enemies, will realize that only in contemporary Rome were so much cowardice and laziness combined with so little diligence in making the necessary preparations for her defense. Her fall has plainly demonstrated how harmful the avaricious, ambitious, and lazy government of modern prelates is to the people. Because of this unique example, too, everyone must realize that human happiness is the most fragile of all things. One need only consider how excessive (a few days before) were the vain and ridiculous ceremonies, the lascivious and idle pleasures of the most reverend cardinals, prelates, and courtiers of the Roman curia. Then let him see that because of such despicable frivolity, they are at present more miserable and unfortunate than any other mortals. It is even more important, however, to know and understand clearly the good habits and the great prudence that are required of anyone who wishes (to the extent that it is conceded to mortals) to preserve his resources, his life, his honor, and his country, and to keep them safe; and I believe these will be made plain to anyone who reads this account with diligence.

ぐつ

LTHOUGH I KNOW how useful it would be, before telling of the destruction of Rome, to run through the original causes of the war, so that the reader could see how the violent actions of men are born and grow and how they are interrelated, nevertheless, I must omit them. During these most tumultuous days for Rome – because of which our country still finds itself in great danger – I never thought to write about things that had occurred in the distant past, but only to note succinctly the principal events from the formation of the League until its dissolution. The sketches for great enterprises are colored in badly, when they are not first measured with diligence and thought through with great intelligence by princes and republics. That was the case with the League. It was started without money, without the leadership essential to such a dangerous undertaking, and lacking the resolve, unity, and appropriate aims necessary to dim the grandeur of an emperor and to liberate Italy from the greed and cruelty of his representatives. The treachery and rapacity of these representatives as well as the power of Caesar are very well known to every Italian, and I will not describe them. But I will describe the structure and purposes of the League. Its unfortunate and pitiable history ought to inspire terror in anyone who would attempt serious actions without considering the luck, strength, and courage of his enemy, with overconfidence in his own forces and an unrealistic approach to setting and achieving his goals.

I must also pass over the negotiations aimed at limiting Caesar's power that the pope, England, and the Venetians held with the government of France, after the cursed and devastating capture of the Most Christian King of France that took place two years ago at Pavia. I shall also leave out the talks that were held with the French king immediately after he was restored to liberty, to convince him that it was neither safe nor honorable for him to uphold the agreement he had made while he was the emperor's prisoner in Spain. They persuaded him instead that without giving up Burgundy, he could force the emperor to return his first-born sons. They argued that Caesar should be stripped of his Italian possessions and confined within the ancient and customary boundaries of the German empire. Nor shall I say anything about the rhetoric by which the Most Christian King concealed his repudiation of the terms of his agreement with Caesar; nor how at last the Imperial Majesty, realizing his error and the treachery of the French king, hastily sent Monseigneur de Bourbon with a very small number of soldiers from Spain to Italy by sea. Caesar named Bourbon his representative and invested him as duke of Milan.

Nor will I write of the clever arguments by which Caesar tried to persuade the pope, England, and the other powers that he desired peace above all else; while at the same time, seeing that no peace was concluded, he was busy gathering men and money. He commandeered all the ships that were in the ports of Spain against the wishes of their captains, so that he could despatch them at need to aid his agents in Italy. I must also omit Pope Clement's fear that Francesco Sforza, the legitimate duke of Milan, would surrender the Castello at Milan to the Spanish, because of the scarcity of supplies and because it might seem to him that he had been abandoned by his allies. To avoid this, against his nature and will, His Holiness was forced to declare war against Caesar. Nor, lastly, shall I describe with what skill and ingenuity, the few imperial forces that were already in Lombardy humiliated and overcame the people of Milan; and how easily and shamefully the riches and the gentlewomen that were in that city became their prey. To do all this would require that I rehearse these and many other events that happened before the outbreak of war.

To describe its origins, if I were to start (as the ancient expression goes) "from the egg," I would carry myself too far from my story. It would then be necessary, to explain the things I now omit, to go still further back into the past, and so I would distance myself more and more from the outbreak of the war. As everyone knows, war and peace, whether simulated or real, are linked together in the affairs of principalities and republics, and one necessarily depends on the other. Anyone who wants to give exhaustive information about one would be forced to write a universal history. Such an undertaking (speaking frankly) is entirely beyond my capacity and the limits of my knowledge.

Of events prior to the formation of the League I shall only record that there were 10,000 imperial troops in Lombardy, consisting of Italians, Spaniards, and Germans, along with 2,000 cavalry. They were garrisoned in Alessandria, Pavia, Cremona, Lodi, and Milan, under the command (after the death of the marquis of Pescara) of his nephew, the marquis of Vasto, and of Antonio de Leva. After the decisive victory at Pavia, these troops maintained control over the duchy of Milan. Because they had not been paid by the emperor, they extorted money ruthlessly from every city and town. Peasants and agricultural workers were treated so brutally and were so thoroughly intimidated by them that very few were to be found at any wages.

Only the fortress at Cremona and the Castello at Milan were still held by Francesco Sforza. He and his retainers had been under siege in the Castello almost since the capture of the Most Christian King of France. Every other town was in the control of the imperial forces; and they kept the Castello carefully and continually guarded to prevent its being resupplied and to keep the duke in their hands. They also controlled Genoa and the greater part of its coast and dominions.

The Venetians had carefully fortified and provisioned their major cities. Having apparently set their immoderate ambition aside, they declared their willingness to cooperate in the liberation of Italy. They pledged their army and a portion of the cost that would be fixed when the League was agreed on. Their aim was to limit the imperial power. The duke of Ferrara, recognizing that he could not come to terms with Clement VII, sent ambassadors to Caesar to negotiate a treaty with His Majesty. The duke of Mantua was unable to come out entirely against the emperor because of feudal obligations to him; but as a soldier of the pope and *gonfaloniere* of the Holy Church, he could not fail to favor the League. The people of Lucca (as had been their custom for many, many years) took no public stance but tried to maintain the friendship of the foreign princes with money.

Because they were extremely discontented with the government of the Medici, the whole of Florence at that time was more in favor of war than peace, believing that in a war the opportunity might arise to liberate themselves from servitude to the Medici. Siena, realizing that the pope intended to return Fabio Petrucci to power, had exiled with violence and near unanimity many citizens of his faction. It was entirely committed to the imperial cause. In Rome, because of the avarice of Cardinal Armellini, the methods of those who advised Clement, and the danger (because of Clement's animosity towards Cardinal Colonna) to the Ghibelline party and the Colonna family, there were many who were ill disposed to His Holiness. In the kingdom of Naples, where Cardinal Colonna and his faction had fled, there was much ill-will expressed towards Pope Clement because of his newly-declared opposition to the emperor. In that kingdom there was no power except the Ghibellines and they easily kept the Guelf party beaten down and oppressed. All Italy, but especially Lombardy – and there principally Genoa and Milan – at that time was suffering a scarcity of every sort of food. This was caused by the continual warfare and the poor harvests in recent years; the famine was apparently only going to be worse in future because the new crop did not look abundant.

This assessment of the situation of the Italian states in general, the duchy of Milan in particular, and of the imperial forces was what provoked the sudden announcement of the Holy League (which was proclaimed under such a venerable title) against the emperor. If the assessment had been different, the League would not have been formed. The manifest discontent of the Lombard peoples and the need for supplies in the Castello of Milan, coupled with the belief that the imperial forces could be deprived of the recent harvest, caused the premature proclamation. Only the forces of the Church and those of the Venetians were assembled, although from hour to hour the arrival of ten thousand Swiss soldiers was expected. The pope (acting under the name of the duke of Milan) had sent the bishop of Lodi with money to have them quickly dispatched into Italy. The Most Christian King of France was expected to quickly send the aid he had promised.

The articles of the League which were published in May of '26 were many, but the following were the most important:

§ The pope, the king of France, the king of England, the Venetians, the duke of Milan, and the other parties were each obligated to contribute at a specified rate to the total expense of the war.

§ War was to be maintained for as long as it took to bring the emperor to an agreement with all the signatories.

§ If Lombardy were retaken it would remain the possession of Francesco Sforza.

§ The kings of England and France would soon declare war on Flanders.

§ Genoa would be besieged, and the kingdom of Naples attacked from the sea by a large communal armada.

§ The Most Christian King of France would quickly dispatch a large army and one of his highest officers, under whose command the forces of the League would be united.

The forces financed by the Church were brought together at Piacenza in preparation for joining up with the Venetian forces at Chiari, a fortress on the north side of the Po River. At this time, Don Ugo of Moncada passed through Lombardy, sent (as it was then supposed) to the pope by Caesar as a stratagem, under pretense of seeking to reach an agreement. The real reason was to encourage the imperial forces, since His Majesty was unable to send additional troops into Italy at that time. Having made his way through France, Don Ugo stopped for a few days in Milan. After promising the imperial forces there that reinforcements would soon be arriving, he set out on the road for Rome. Near Bologna he came upon Count Guido Rangoni, Signor Vitello Vitelli, and other officers of the Church with substantial numbers of infantry and horse. And, indeed, wherever he went, he became aware of some part of the great preparations that were being made against Caesar.

After he passed through Florence, he arrived at Siena, and having reassured the Sienese, he wrote several letters to the emperor, informing him of the dangers that his soldiers were facing in Lombardy and throughout Italy and urging him to come to terms with the League. He declared that he saw no other hope of safety for Caesar's men, nor any other way to preserve the territories that had already been acquired in Italy. From these letters and others from the principal officers of the Spanish forces at Milan, which were afterwards intercepted, the fears of the imperial forces became known.

Nonetheless, the imperial officers who were in Lombardy, once they knew that war was inevitable, quickly brought the forces that had been dispersed in various places together around Pavia and Milan, although they were careful to leave Alessandria and Cremona well guarded. They stationed about eight hundred Italian infantry in Lodi, and with all possible speed they had as many supplies as they could brought to these cities. They took pains to conceal in which city they intended to take refuge, should the enemy army prove superior in the field. Despite their activity, however, even apart from the intercepted letters, it was obvious from many other signs that they wanted to reach an agreement. Knowing that they had no commission from Caesar to attempt one, they made a point, as is the Spanish custom, despite their fear, always to display great eagerness for battle. Little by little, surreptitiously and with the least possible disclosure of their plans, they brought more forces together in Milan than elsewhere. These troops would permit them to make their stand in that city and also to control the frequent outbreaks caused by the discontent of the Milanese people. I cannot here describe in detail how the people, seeing no way to defend themselves from this cruel occupation, were forced at last to yield to the insolent wishes of their enemies.

Not long after the Spanish troops took up their position in Milan, Francesco Guicciardini arrived at Piacenza, having been sent there by the pope as his lieutenant-general. Giovanni de' Medici and other officers of the Church forces with 600 lancers and 8,000 infantry were there already. They were awaiting a reply from Francesco Maria della Rovere, duke of Urbino, about where and when he and his army would be joining with them. The duke with all the forces of the Venetians was quartered at Chiari. He informed the officers of the Church that he intended to wait for 3,000 additional Swiss mercenaries, because the promised number had not yet arrived at

Belinzona. The bishop of Lodi, having been dispatched, as I said, to recruit 10,000 of them, had been met by their usual greed and insolence and did not have enough money to persuade them.

At this time, Signor Malatesta Baglioni, a Venetian officer, gained entry to Lodi during the night through an arrangement worked out with Messer Ludovico Vistarini, a gentleman of that city. Having killed about sixty soldiers assigned to guard one of the gates, he finally became master of the rest; and it was easy for him to awaken all the rest of the Italian soldiers. He kept the leaders of the occupying troops with him as prisoners. The castello, though, remained in imperial hands. When the Spanish troops at Milan learned what had happened, a contingent of them quickly marched with the marquis of Vasto to Lodi to see if they could recover the city. At first not much resistance was put up, and part of their cavalry easily entered the city. They continued to drive the Venetian infantry back and were forcing them to retreat toward the central piazza. Nonetheless, it seemed to the marquis and his officers that it was turning out to be more difficult and more time-consuming to recapture the city than they had estimated. Fearing to be trapped if Francesco Maria were to counterattack quickly (as seemed likely), they retreated to Milan. After their retreat, the surrender of the castello was negotiated.

This sort of case frequently occurs in military affairs and in many other human actions: the enemy does not always do what is best or what reason would dictate, either through fear or failure to see far enough ahead. But the leader in these situations must take the safest and most prudent course. He cannot always assume that his enemy will fall short in its response, unless he has learned through experience something about his enemy's true nature. Therefore the imperial troops were right to retreat, although many people at that time, judging from effects and not causes, were convinced that they were wrong. It only became clear afterwards that if they had continued the attack, they would have regained Lodi as easily as they had lost it. The duke of Urbino delayed two whole days before going there; and he would not have gone even then, if he had not been spurred on several times by the Venetian quartermaster-general. The cause of his delay, which was not evident then, will be clearly revealed in his future actions.

The capture of Lodi was so important a victory that it convinced the lieutenant-general and all the other officers of the Church to move their troops across the Po. Without waiting any longer for a response from Francesco Maria, they positioned their armies at a distance of three miles from his. Since he was captain-general of the Venetian forces, the command of the League army was placed on his shoulders alone until the commander promised by the Most Christian King of France should arrive. After much discussion the officers of the League agreed that they should waste no further time before attacking Milan. They reasoned that the enemy might abandon the city voluntarily – since there were no more than 7,000 infantry and 400 cavalry including both Spaniards and Germans. Were they to resist, it would be very difficult for them to defend such a large circuit of walls and trenches. In order to defend themselves from attack and hold the Milanese population in check, they would have to divide their forces, leaving some to surround the Castello, and some in various locations within the city, and the remainder at the walls. It was assumed that when battle was joined from several directions at once (as they planned), the people of Milan would give a further advantage to the forces that were trying to liberate them by rebelling.

These judgments easily persuaded the army and brought them full of confidence to Marignano, a fortress ten miles from Milan, with the intention of marching further the next day. The forces of the League comprised

20,000 infantry, including 8,000 artillerymen and arque-busiers, plus 1,500 lancers and a equal number of cavalry. There was also sufficient heavy artillery and field artillery; and the troops were well supplied with food and munitions. Nonetheless the duke halted to await the 3,000 Swiss soldiers, declaring that it was unsafe to leave Marignano without them. He said he was prompted in this judgment by his many experiences with the aggressiveness of the Spanish; indeed he had recovered his dukedom with a small number of them against a large Italian army. From this he had learned that Italian infantry was of no value against the Spanish.

Now it is easy to judge how much His Excellency was in error in this matter, when you consider the well-known fact that not only the quality of an army but victory itself depend on the courage and prudence of the commander. The Romans often observed that the same legions fighting the same enemy achieved outstanding success or ludicrous failure in direct proportion to the quality of those who commanded them. It is also true that if any nationality deserves praise for the practice of arms, whether for skill, cunning, courage or endurance, or for outstanding successes in past centuries, there is none to compare with the Italians. And if in our own time we see Italian soldiers overwhelmed and beaten down, this does not reflect poor military ability, but the lack of captains who could mold them and bring out their natural, age-old aggressiveness. All those who have written about military science have proved by a variety of arguments that the courage or indifference of the commander is of primary importance in an army. This is perhaps best illustrated by an analogy, based on long experience, that states: the army that is like deer, disciplined and trained by one who is like a lion, will always do better than soldiers who are like lions led by a deer. But Francesco Maria, who was, either through excessive caution or by nature, adverse to dangers and difficulties and therefore unwilling to advance, put the blame on men who did not deserve it. Finally, though, urged and spurred on by the arguments of the lieutenant-general and the eagerness of Giovanni de' Medici, who argued more strongly than the others for the advance, the army marched to Castello San Donato, four miles closer to Milan.

Some time before this, Monseigneur de Bourbon had entered that city with three hundred Spanish troops. Bourbon was very angry because he had not learned until their arrival in Genoa of the serious situation facing the imperial forces in Lombardy. Forced to make a virtue of necessity, and disguising his own uneasiness (as a commander must), Bourbon encouraged his men, swearing to them that there was a huge force in Spain ready to depart as soon as the winds were favorable; and that he had been promised that within a short time additional troops would be coming to their aid from Germany via Genoa. Because he had recently been named by Caesar as the new duke of Milan, he was very friendly and encouraging to the people and nobles, giving them hope that he would govern them justly and benignly in the future. He thanked everyone on behalf of the emperor for the allegiance that they had shown to His Majesty, promising that soon it would be richly rewarded. On the other hand, he did not neglect to put into effect with speed everything that was necessary for the defense of the city. To keep the more spirited and courageous Milanese in a state of apprehension, he had rumors spread that they had promised money to the Italian soldiers if they would liberate the city.

While Bourbon was losing no time in doing what was necessary to keep the state that he had received as a gift from Caesar, the army of the League left San Donato and arrived in San Martino, three and a half miles from Milan. The reason that they marched such a short distance in a day was because the duke of Urbino (even though all the officers in the army were eager to besiege Milan) absolutely insisted on having the three thousand Swiss before he would attack the city. Five companies of them did arrive later, and another five were expected in a short time. At this point, Francesco Maria heard from certain of his special spies that the enemy were saying that when he and his army attacked, they intended to withdraw immediately to Pavia through the gate on the opposite side of the city. They were supposed to be keeping their baggage and carriages ready so that they could evacuate whenever they chose.

Francesco Maria was completely persuaded by their story. While he had always insisted before that he would not attack Milan without the three thousand Swiss, he suddenly moved out without informing his officers of the reason for his change of plans. Then, having led his men to the walls in the area outside Porta Tosa, he failed to set up camp at the place repeatedly designated in the staff conferences. He also ignored the plan of battle that had been worked out by all the officers. Carried away by hope, he presented himself, as I have said, at the walls of Milan, with no plan or any order for giving battle, if necessary, or for intimidating the enemy. He believed far too easily that what his spies had convinced him of would immediately happen.

After waiting aimlessly for several hours, with all his soldiers in arms and unfed, he began to realize that his plans were coming to nothing. Finally, after midday he ordered four cannon to be positioned a little distance away in the areas outside Porta Tosa and Porta Romana, where he intended to attack. Because they had not been put into position earlier, as they should have been, their placement caused great confusion in the army, and greatly increased the confidence of the enemy. The imperial soldiers showed in every possible way that they intended to defend not only the city but the suburbs as well, because they knew that they would always have time to retreat to Pavia when they needed to. They knew that whenever an enemy enters a city taken by force, their only concern is looting, not chasing after those who abandon it in flight. The duke, though, failed to realize or to plan for the fact that armed with this hope, the Spaniards would put up very heavy resistance before retreating.

As evening approached, His Excellency Francesco Maria found himself stymied. With his army worn out and in disarray, he was forced to accept the shelter at hand, promising his men that on the following morning at dawn, they would attack in better order. The men had to sleep out in the open or against the walls in great discomfort. Nonetheless, the knowledge that in the morning they were going to try and take Milan made them willing to accept so much discomfort and disorder.

Realizing the feeble and ill-conceived nature of the attack, the imperial forces fired repeated shots towards the camp, and not in vain. Several times during the night they sent out small bands, forcing the soldiers of the League to arm and preventing them from sleeping. These tactics frightened the duke so much that before midnight he decided to break camp and to retreat with all his forces, but only as far as San Martino (as his Excellency then declared).

Learning of his decision and not being able to hold him back, the Venetian quartermaster-general immediately went to find the lieutenant-general and inform him of the duke's plan. When the lieutenant-general heard of the duke's sudden change of heart, he immediately left his quarters and went with Signor Giovanni and some other officers to see if he could dissuade the duke from this hasty retreat. When they reached him, they found that he was absolutely determined to move his army. He had, in fact, already sent the artillery and his carriages on ahead and given orders for the entire army to retreat immediately. In the face of this impulsiveness, the lieutenant-general tried every possible means to persuade him, using arguments and reasons that should have kept him from running away. Recognizing at last that he could not convince him, he began to complain and to protest to His Excellency that he would swear before all his colleagues that such a shameful flight was not only against all reason but very likely to lead to chaos and disaster in the future.

Francesco Maria did not change his mind; on the contrary, with greater insistence than before he urged the foot soldiers and cavalry to retreat. He didn't pause until he reached Marignano, and he would not have stopped there either (since the artillery had already gone a league beyond the place he had ordered them to), if the renewed complaints of the lieutenant-general and the opposition of the other lords and officers had not made him change his mind. It had been his intention, they then learned, to return to Lodi, because (as he often said) he had so little confidence in Italian infantry. Such words and actions were certainly ill-advised; because of them the courage of his own men was diminished and that of the enemy increased.

It was then the common opinion that had His Excellency remained for a few days laying siege to Milan, and encamped at the place repeatedly designated in the staff conferences, that the Spanish, beset by fear of the Milanese people, of the forces in the Castello, and of those outside the walls, coupled with their increasing need for supplies, would have retreated to Pavia of their own volition.

Anyone who had doubts about the courage or prudence of the duke could resolve them entirely by considering this retreat. The duke should never have attacked Milan on the basis of such unreliable intelligence, especially since, as he often repeated, he didn't have confidence in his troops. Once there, though, he should have remained for a few days, since he could have done so without danger, as many will absolutely affirm. But His

Excellency, for some unknown reason, fled to Marignano at night and in complete disorder. If it weren't for the fact that Signor Giovanni and the men of his Black Bands remained alone at the walls (although against the duke's advice) as a rear guard, the army of the League would have felt the enemy's heat with very grave results. Hearing the noise of the army breaking camp, large numbers of enemy troops came out of the city. They were easily contained, though, and driven back inside by the ferocity of the Black Bands, who had no intention of leaving Milan before daybreak. Then, in good order and with high spirits, they followed in the footsteps of the terrified army, underscoring the duke's timidity by their courage and panache.

Not long after the duke's retreat to Marignano, five thousand Swiss in several companies arrived to join the army of the League. With these increased forces Francesco Maria was strong enough to meet the enemy wherever he chose, and having no excuse for further delay, he decided to regain part of his lost honor by coming to the aid of the Castello, which was in extreme need of supplies. To this end he held daily conferences to determine the best plan to follow for bringing aid to the besieged Castello and liberating Milan from its cruel occupation.

While the army continued in these long and fruitless discussions and used up time without gaining anything, about four hundred "useless mouths" arrived in Marignano. These were mostly women who had been sent out of the Castello by Francesco Sforza, duke of Milan, because they could no longer be fed. They described to Francesco Maria and the other officers the extreme need in which they had left their besieged lord, and how easily he could be relieved. They said that he was encircled only by a trench, which they had crossed over without difficulty, even though it was a rainy night. On behalf of the duke of Milan, they declared that if the army intended to save the Castello, they must reprovision it within four days. Otherwise, the duke would be forced to take measures that only the most extreme necessity could compel. With the advice and counsel of all the leaders, the army took up new positions about two miles from the walls of Milan at a place called Cassarate.

There, once again, they delayed, putting additional time into reconnaissance and new consultations. At last they decided that within two days they would attempt to resupply the Castello and to divert the siege forces by attacking the outskirts of Milan. They did not, however, communicate their plans (as they should have) to Francesco Sforza, who had, after all, many times awaited help in vain. With nothing in the Castello left to live on, and ignorant of the army's plan, or even of its position, Francesco Sforza was forced to surrender the Castello to Monseigneur de Bourbon. The people within and their belongings were to be respected, and certain other conditions of no great importance (which were not in any case observed) were agreed on; and accompanied by those who had remained faithful to him during the long siege, Francesco Sforza departed for Cassarate.

The loss of the Castello was a serious setback, and its sole cause was the duke's procrastination. This is especially clear if one considers the words he used in public when he received the news. When His Excellency heard that the Castello had capitulated and that within a few hours it would be in the hands of the Spanish, he said in the presence of the lieutenant-general and several other officers, who were still arguing among themselves about how and when to relieve it, "This loss of the Castello is very serious for the duke of Milan, but for our purposes it is more beneficial than harmful. We were under an obligation to attempt to resupply it, which we clearly could not have done without the gravest risk; it would have been our ruin." These were words that gave the clearest indication of the prospects for victory in the future.

Apart from this, but on the very same day, Francesco Maria informed the lieutenant-general that unless he was made captain-general of the whole League, he would not continue to serve. One can easily imagine how welcome this must have been to the pope and the Venetians, given the views of the lieutenant-general and the quartermaster-general who were both convinced that it was entirely the duke's fault that a crucial fortress had fallen into the hands of the enemy. Nonetheless, to avoid exasperating Francesco Maria, since it was impossible to find a quick replacement for him at that time, response was given to him via the lieutenant-general that since the League hoped that the duke of Ferrara would soon come to terms or that someone would be coming from France with the forces of the Most Christian King to whom this title could not be denied, they could not take that course at this time; but should neither eventuality come about, they would not fail to honor his request.

The events that have occurred up to this point demonstrate clearly how important it is in major campaigns to have an outstanding commander. In those cases, which frequently arise, where one cannot be found, it would be wiser to avoid situations of manifest danger. Rather, with means other than war, if possible, postpone the realization of your goals or forestall your ruin. And wait for a better opportunity. If in extreme peril you cannot find an able commander, persuade yourself that you will be harmed less by your enemies if you don't oppose yourself to their force, than if, relying on vain hopes, you provoke them against you with greater hatred. Having no way to placate them, await their wrath with the resignation that comes from knowing there is nothing more that can be done.

On the same day that the Castello of Milan surrendered to Bourbon, a shameful attempt was made by men under orders from the pope and his counselors (although against the advice of those in Florence who were consulted) using Florentine artillery to return the Sienese exiles to power. These forces were routed and put to flight at night by a very small number of Sienese, thanks to the outstanding officers both of the Church and of Florence who were present. These men underestimated their enemy; they trusted entirely and unwisely in the integrity of the exiles; they let their soldiers run wild and pillage the countryside at will and take their spoils up to the city walls to sell them. Though they knew better, they acted like men ignorant of military order and regulations; and it is no wonder that they dishonored themselves and those who had sent them.

After the loss of the Castello, the duke of Urbino fortified the camp at Cassarate, and surrounded it with very impressive moats and earthworks. Then he did nothing for fifty days. And if during this time the people of Milan didn't rebel or show that they wanted to be free from occupation, they should not be criticized or blamed for that, since they were not aided in any way by the forces of the League. In fact, since the Spanish had had sufficient time to overawe them, they were so thoroughly intimidated that no one was eager to leave his own house, let alone to run armed through the streets in order to liberate himself.

The Milanese people aren't the only example that shows how little resistance an unarmed population, without any experience and without a leader, can make against an occupying army with all the means to rule others by force. Only the Black Bands (so-called from the color of their insignia) because of the skill and courage of Signor Giovanni, who led them, showed themselves continually willing to meet the enemy face to face. They often rode up to the walls of Milan, where they skirmished with the imperial troops, and they always triumphed even when they went up against Spaniards or Germans in equal or greater numbers. They were the only ones that the imperial forces within were afraid of.

Consequently many Spaniards (as many people will confirm) armed with arquebuses came outside the walls determined to die themselves or to kill Signor Giovanni.

In these attacks he displayed not only outstanding leadership but courage and audacity as well. These are qualities that are rarely combined in one man. An insightful man is often cautious because of the many risks that he foresees. Courage, which in many cases seems to be accompanied by intellectual weakness, is often characterized by recklessness. Because of these repeated successes, Signor Giovanni always argued in staff conferences that Milan should be stormed. He volunteered his troops and himself as a vanguard in the attack, and he wanted to be the first to enter the besieged city. Francesco Maria, however, was bound and determined not to fight or to take any risks whatsoever; and he often insisted that the more prudent way to win was with the sword in its scabbard. He argued repeatedly that because of the difficulty of finding provisions, the imperial forces would be forced to abandon the city in a few days.

Now this is a strategy that was recommended from time to time by some of the Ancients. In this case it was neither wise nor certain, however, because a long siege exposed the League itself to several dangers: help could come to the besieged; one of the allies could run out of money; incidents might arise among allies with so many different natures and goals that would destroy the opportunity that then presented itself. Consequently it would have been more sensible to attack from several directions at once, and risk the loss of a few hundred of his soldiers. Because, if Milan were captured, the war would be ended in large part if not entirely. If they tried but failed to take it, the League would not be in any worse situation than if they hadn't tried.

The duke was convinced and so were those in Rome that drawing out the siege would either wear down and demoralize the enemy (especially since they weren't being paid by the emperor), or that the difficulty of obtaining supplies would force them to leave. But this was a miscalculation, since the Spanish and Germans in fact lacked nothing. They held captive a very rich city, well stocked with every sort of commodity. In fact, provisions were being brought into the city every day in any way possible. And though the people of Milan were suffering from lack of food, they were obliged to be patient, and to endure the surpassing greed, lust, and cruelty of the enemy. Besides, even though Francesco Maria was camped within two miles of Milan, he made no effort and took no care to intercept the food supplies that were continually brought into the city from every direction. He should have done that if, as he maintained, he intended to take the city by siege.

By this point in the war, Genoa had been besieged for some time by the galleys of the pope, the French, and the Venetians; and the Genoese had lost many of the ships and boats that brought provisions to the city. They were reduced to such a state that if they had not been resupplied by land, they would have had to send the white flag to Andrea Doria, captain-general of the armada. Therefore it was decided to send enough soldiers of the League to cut off food supplies from the land-side; and Francesco Maria agreed to dispatch them whenever new Swiss soldiers, who were expected any day, should arrive.

While the army remained at Cassarate with these hopes and plans, the Venetians judged the time was right to attempt to capture Cremona. They argued that it would be easy to take the city, and that this would hamper the enemy and lessen his confidence. It would be especially beneficial in that it would impede the passage of new lancers from Germany, who were beginning to cause a certain amount of apprehension. It would also increase the security of Venice and of the Church territories. This campaign was strongly supported by Francesco Maria, not only to satisfy the wishes of those who were paying him, but also to free himself from other demands by adopting this new plan. (In this he was acting like a man who puts himself at risk through excessive caution.) He believed that it would be easy to capture this city since the castello was in the hands of the League already, and since there were no more than 1,000 imperial soldiers and 200 cavalry (both Spanish and German together), who were hated by the population.

Malatesta Baglioni in command of about 5,000 infantry and 600 cavalry was sent there. After several days, however, he had achieved nothing except to show the enemy with several artillery barrages where their weak points were and then give them time to reinforce them. Since he no longer thought it safe to attack the city, he wrote to the duke that he did not have sufficient forces to guarantee victory. Even after fresh troops were sent to him by the duke, he still had gained nothing. Finally, to avoid further loss of time, it seemed necessary to His Excellency to go there himself with a substantial number of soldiers. After earthworks and trenches were constructed and the walls had been attacked from different directions, the Germans and Spaniards, who had defended themselves so bravely up to this point, were obliged to surrender on condition of saving their lives and their goods. The Germans agreed to return by the shortest route to Germany and the Spaniards by the road through the Marches (Le Marche) to the kingdom of Naples.

Many people condemned the terms of this surrender with good reason, since the enemy were few, poorly armed, and surrounded by a hostile populace. In addition, the inner fortress was strongly defended against them. They could not possibly have held out against attack from so many directions. How good it would have been for the League to regain its lost honor by capturing such an important city for itself and cutting to pieces, as military practice requires, such inveterate and cruel enemies of Italy. But since it doesn't seem wise to me always (like

Momus) to be blaming and condemning errors which must be obvious to anyone, I will say only that the tragic fate of Italy always seemed to force this duke to choose the worst possible course of action. The Spaniards who maintained that they intended to embark for the kingdom, once they reached Carpi, made themselves masters of that city in a few days. From there they did great damage to the territory of the League. The Germans, who returned safe and rich to their country, gave great encouragement to those who intended to come or were scheduled to come into Italy; and the majority of them volunteered to return to seek vengeance for the "injuries" they had received!

While the surrender was being negotiated at Cremona, the marquis of Saluzzo, who had been sent by the Most Christian King of France, finally arrived in Astigniano with 500 lancers and 6,000 soldiers. Another 2,000 Swiss arrived in Cassarate; and 2,000 more were expected in a short time. Once the campaign at Cremona was over, the duke of Urbino intended to position himself and his army between Pavia and Milan in order to restrict the provisioning of the enemy more effectively. He was also keeping the Genoese campaign in mind. These were very laudable and useful plans, which he could certainly have carried out at that time. Nonetheless he postponed the execution of these and many other projects, which were brought up in the staff conferences every day by the commanders, while he allowed the imperial forces to delay their retreat from Cremona.

While His Excellency was letting this opportunity slip through his fingers, a disastrous and outrageous attack took place in Rome. The pope had been warned many times by those who were concerned for his safety that he must remain well armed and vigilant against both Colonna treachery and Spanish deceit. His Holiness, however, was persuaded by someone who had great influence with him that these fears were groundless and that there was no need to spend money on defense. Completely unprotected, he was attacked by Cardinal Colonna and Don Ugo of Moncada with four hundred horsemen. His Holiness quickly fled to Castel Sant' Angelo with many of his supporters, urged on by the importunity of others more than by fear for himself. The castello was unarmed and, it was also reported, without provisions or anything else necessary to its defense (as the fortresses of the Church generally are). When the Roman people failed to take up arms in his support, Clement was obliged to accede to the insolent demands of a small number of his enemies. He agreed to suspend hostilities for six months and to order the withdrawal of his troops south of the Po. To speed the enemy's departure from Rome, the pope offered Jacopo Salviati, or one of his sons, together with Filippo Strozzi as hostages. The Colonna and the Spanish were thus assured that he intended to fulfill what he had agreed to under duress.

After looting Saint Peter's, the papal palace, and the residences of various cardinals, shamefully and without any reverence for religion, the troops departed loaded with spoils. They took with them Filippo Strozzi alone, since they had accepted 30,000 scudi as security for Jacopo Salviati. They quickly dispersed into various fortified towns of theirs near Rome. This sack was truly unprecedented and a foreshadowing and presage of the greater ruin to come. It is entirely indicative of how the Imperial Majesty, or better yet the imperial Fortune, beguiles the enemies of Charles V with the hope of quick and easy victory and then with some new and unanticipated event, it reduces them to chaos and disaster.

Because of this unexpected and bizarre event, all the many plans of the League that were described above became null and void. By commission of the pope (who intended to keep the faith he had pledged), the lieutenant-general sent Vitello Vitelli with his cavalry and two thousand Swiss to Rome, and the lieutenant-general himself retreated to Piacenza with the other forces paid for by the Church and the Florentines. These movements created uncertainty in the minds of the other officers of the League concerning the future of the alliance. This concern was aggravated when Francesco Maria made no effort to leave Cremona. In fact (as many then affirmed) he was away visiting his consort, the duchess at Mantua. This caused many of the officers who were at Cassarate with the rest of the army of the League to complain repeatedly of the duke's negligence.

When the marquis of Saluzzo and the two thousand Swiss who had been expected finally arrived, the French and the Venetians, very strongly supported by Giovanni de' Medici, decided to carry on with the war. They planned no change in their position for now unless conditions changed; and they hoped that the pope would not have to honor the agreement he had made under duress. The two thousand Swiss were on their way to Rome with Signor Vitello, and all the forces of the Church and of Florence were with the lieutenant-general at Piacenza, except for those that were sent from there to Parma under Count Guido Rangoni. Those remaining at Cassarate finally got the duke of Urbino to return. There they awaited together the decisions of the French and Venetian governments about what they were to do. And while the army waited without making plans or indeed doing anything at all, the pope attacked the Colonna with nothing but censures and excommunications, even though they had violated the conditions of an agreement made a short while before the attack, and their followers and dependents had pillaged sacred places and carried off precious relics.

At this time it was learned that twelve thousand Lutherans had arrived in Italy, recruited for the emperor and commanded by George von Frundsberg. He was of noble blood, very experienced in the wars in Lombardy, and a close friend of Bourbon. Each soldier had received one scudo from the private fortune of their commander, who was one of the leaders of the Lutheran sect. No one had known which road they would be taking for Milan, and consequently many passes were guarded by the men of the Grisone region on behalf of the League. They had been ordered to fortify certain places, since it was believed that such a large force could only cross into Italy on main roads rather than paths or byways. At word of their arrival, Signor Giovanni with his Black Bands left the camp at Cassarate with the intention of engaging them if he could. The duke of Urbino followed with part of the army in the direction of Cremona, more to secure the Venetian frontier than to aid the Black Bands.

The reason that these troops had not arrived in Italy earlier (as the imperials intended) was in part because of difficulties of payment, but primarily because of the invasion of Hungary two months before by an enormous army led by the Grand Turk himself. This attack had alarmed the Archduke Ferdinand, brother of the emperor. And indeed the infidels were streaming through Hungary looting and burning almost the whole country. They had routed and scattered the Hungarian army at Mohács, where they had come against them. Lajos, their king, had been drowned in a huge ditch near the Danube, when he tried to wade it as he fled with a few of his men. The Turks were approaching to within a few miles of Vienna, the principal and wealthiest city of the archduke. His Majesty King Ferdinand was obliged to see to his own defense and forget the affairs of Italy.

Finally, however, the Turkish army began to retreat towards Constantinople, loaded down with untold plunder and an incredible quantity of prisoners. Whether this was because of the extremely cold season that had begun, or because of some new and terrible illness that broke out among the troops is not known. They left Körös, Strem, and Beograd well guarded; these cities had been captured without much effort during the war, though by their nature they were very secure. They would prove very useful for further harassment of Hungary.

After the retreat of the Turkish army, the archduke, eager to make up for lost time, saw to the departure of the Germans for Italy under Captain George with the greatest diligence and speed. Indeed, no sooner had their departure been heard of, than their arrival at Castiglione degli Strivieri in the territory of Mantua became known. They had come down by an entirely different route from the one which had seemed most likely in the deliberations of the League and elsewhere.

And this is what happens to those who convince themselves that they can contain the enemy where the passes are steepest. They don't consider how many other places the enemy can use when they meet resistance in one of them. Not far away there is bound to be a route that is easier and safer for them. With their infantry in the lead, they climb over the steep and seemingly inaccessible mountains, and descend to deep, unguarded valleys. And it is that much more difficult to contain them because their opponent has to divide his forces among all the narrow and steep places. Where these men are few, they are insufficient, and when they are sufficient, it is safer and more praiseworthy to make an attack with the entire force together against the enemy. Countries that are difficult to travel in are more useful to those who have no cavalry and fewer troops than the enemy. When they are forced to close combat, they can avoid being surrounded while fighting, and they can always retreat for their safety.

I could give many examples of deep and wide rivers or of steep and rugged mountains and valleys that armies have crossed, since ancient histories are full of them. Such examples would show how ill-founded the modern strategy is, even though it is deeply ingrained in those with a reputation for wisdom in our time. Nonetheless I will give only one example: the crossing of the Alps in '15 by the French army, led by the Most Christian King, who is still living, with a very great number of horses and heavy artillery. This would be a difficult force to lead even through wide and well-populated plains, let alone through the narrow, uninhabited, and obstacle-filled Alps. Even though the mountains were guarded by the Swiss, who are very well prepared to defend them since they are native to mountainous places, these mountaineers could not prevent the passage of the French by an unguarded route into Lombardy, even though they were slowed down by a multitude of loaded carts and other equipment even larger. But in order to avoid too long a digression, I will reserve with other subjects until a more convenient time the many reasons and examples that could be adduced to counter the modern opinion. Let it suffice for the present to have pointed out how false and therefore dangerous is the hope of those who make holding the passes against the enemy the mainstay of their defense.

Therefore, returning to my subject, I say that when Signor Giovanni had learned where the lancers had descended into Italy, he and his Black Bands immediately began moving towards them prepared to attack. He knew that they were without field artillery and very badly armed. Signor Giovanni set out, leaving Francesco Maria very far behind.

Encountering the Germans in a confined area known as the "Seraglio of Mantua," he assaulted them with such energy that he forced them continually to retreat towards Govérnolo, a fortified town at the confluence of the Mincio and Po rivers. In a short time he had weakened them so much that he could reasonably hope for victory over them in the near future. One evening as he was returning to his camp near Borgoforte, he was mortally wounded by a musket shot in the leg near the knee. He was carried to Mantua, where he died in great anguish a few days later from that terrible wound.

This was a very devastating loss because it left this poor
Italy of ours (let it be said with due respect for all the
other Italian officers) entirely at the mercy of the foreigners. Our city, ironically, was liberated from a long-
standing fear inspired by his courage and aggressiveness.
And even though he was arrogant and very dedicated to
venereal things, nonetheless his liberality, tolerance, courage, and experience as a master of arms were unequaled.
Had King Philip of Macedon or Hamilcar of Carthage
been his father, or had he been born in Rome in those
days when the training of military men had been per-
fected, he would not have proved inferior to Alexander,
or Hannibal, or Scipio, or any other of the ancient
Roman generals (even though they were most excellent
and most aggressive). In a time so corrupted, and in an
army so timid and disorganized, by age twenty-eight he
had gained a reputation for himself by his own talent
that exceeded every other. As soon as his death became
known to the Spanish and Germans troops fighting in
various parts of Italy, they expressed the most extraordinary relief, for they had known him through long
experience as friend and enemy both, and they rated him
far above every other officer.

The allies meanwhile began to lose confidence because
of such a great and unexpected loss. Their apprehension
was increased by the arrival at Porto Santo Stefano, near
Siena, of part of the army of Charles V, led from Spain by
Charles de Lannoy, viceroy of Naples. This army had been
scattered by Andrea Doria, when it first attempted to
cross from Corsica to Genoa. It did not remain long at
Porto S. Stefano, either. Instead it fled to Gaeta, because
Doria was preparing to attack the Sienese port. The number of soldiers brought over from Spain totaled less than
6,000. There were about 2,000 Germans among them
who had been fighting for several years on the borders of
France and Spain; they were considered to be the back-
bone of the army. Their departure for Italy had been

delayed for so long because the emperor had been using them to make war on the Moors of Grenada, who refused to be rebaptized and to pay a sum of money well beyond their usual amount. When the viceroy arrived at Gaeta, he had his infantry disembark. Either because of the conditions at sea, or the change of air, or for some other reason, the majority of them, especially the Germans, became ill. Though not many died, they were so debilitated, or in a manner of speaking, so shaken up, that they couldn't march.

At this time the pope and the other Italian allies were making every effort to convince the Most Christian King and the king of England of the serious situation facing the forces of the League. Because of the arrival of the new lancers, the death of Signor Giovanni, and the army newly disembarked at Gaeta, they needed to provide it quickly with new Swiss mercenaries. No other help could arrive soon enough or in sufficient numbers to counteract the strong blows from Fortune that they had sustained in such a short period of time. Using various arguments, they tried to convince both kings that unless help came quickly and in great quantity, it would be too late, and the war would be brought into their home territories. Then it would no longer be a question of limiting Caesar's power, but of their own survival. These factors seemed very significant to both kings, and induced them to promise that they would quickly send help so that the League could guarantee the security of the Italian states. Nonetheless nothing was done at that time. Many reasons for such negligence and miscalculation were advanced, but the most significant were these: among the French, over-confidence and the scarcity of funds; among the English, the belief that the emperor would accept a general treaty. In order to avoid a final break with England, the Imperial Majesty skillfully maintained the hopes of Cardinal Wolsey, by showing a desire for peace of which the emperor himself would be the author. This is an example that shows clearly what happens to states which in their greatest need must depend on help from friends and allies who are far away, or from those who do not believe that they could ever find themselves in similar danger.

A short time after the mortal wounding of Signor Giovanni, Captain George von Frundsberg led his Germans cross the Po in safety. They had marched along the river through the territory of Ferrara and of the Church in incredible discomfort caused by heavy rains and an extreme scarcity of food supplies. They remained for four months then in Castel S. Giovanni and Borgo S. Donnino, towns near Piacenza. There they did no other damage than to destroy the images in the churches and cast the holy relics to the ground along with all the sacraments except for the Eucharist. For this alone these Lutherans showed reverence. But the other things that with good reason the modern Church reveres are despised by the Lutheran sect, and they broke them to pieces and trod them underfoot. (I will write about the beliefs, customs, and origins of the Lutherans in detail in another more suitable time and place.)

These newly arrived Germans were obliged to live off the country, and they protested to those who brought them provisions that they wanted to unite their force with the imperial soldiers in Milan. Then all together they could move more securely into Tuscany. But even after the death of Signor Giovanni, the soldiers in Milan still would not agree to join forces with the new lancers, even though they were told continually by their Spanish officers that they should not waste the opportunity created by his death. Nonetheless their urging was in vain. The soldiers at Milan insisted that they would not set out until they received the outstanding wages they were owed. This was in addition to the two allotments they had received shortly before. Certainly military strategy (which consists primarily in knowing how to take immediate advantage of opportunities which rarely present themselves) would suggest that if the troops from Milan had been united with the newly arrived Lutherans, and if they had immediately crossed the Apennines by the Giogo Pass, they would have routed the forces of the League. After the death of Signor Giovanni the troops of the League were completely demoralized. But delay and division among the imperial army, as they had many times before, gave the League forces time to regroup and regain courage.

Immediately upon the death of Signor Giovanni, the men of the Black Bands were already beginning to disperse. To counteract this, the lieutenant-general gave them money on behalf of the pope and sent part of them quickly to Parma. He was already there, although he had, of course, left Piacenza well garrisoned. He sent the rest of the Black Bands towards Rome, because of fear of the army at Gaeta. He distributed the rest of the forces paid for by the Church and the Florentines between Bologna and Modena. He did this despite the fact that prudence might dictate that all the men of the League be combined and encamped near the enemy to keep pressure on them and to increase their uncertainty. Had this been done, the new lancers would undoubtedly have been forced to recross the Po and march towards Milan. Having less to live on there, and lacking money because they hadn't been paid, it seemed likely that dissension would arise between the two armies. (Unless, of course, the imperial troops of Milan came to terms with the Germans. Had these armies combined, they would have been masters of the countryside everywhere.) But the poverty of the new lancers and their great numbers caused too much anxiety in the troops at Milan, who wanted above all to receive their back pay. They feared the new lancers because they were themselves relatively rich and in inferior numbers, and so it seemed unlikely to many that they would consent to joining forces.

In any case, Francesco Maria would never agree to reunite all the forces of the League. He would not consent to cross the Po with them either, for fear that he would be forced to join battle against his will. And in order to keep the forces of the French and the Swiss under his direct control, he pretended to be afraid that the Venetian territories would be attacked from the northeast. He pledged to release these troops, however, as soon as the enemy had committed himself by marching either towards Bologna or Pontrémoli. This move of his would allow the Venetians to save their men and secure their borders by distancing the war from their territory. Because the Venetians, as always, desired to weaken and harass the other states of Italy, they gladly agreed to the duke's views in hopes that the enemy would march on Tuscany.

Florence meanwhile was in a state of great apprehension and uneasiness and there began to be some enlistment of soldiers. Because the cardinal of Cortona feared that the people might rise up against the government, and because of the fear of external attack, he ordered the walls to be fortified in several parts of the city. Many experts, including Count Pietro Novarro, had been consulted and they had offered plans for fortifying the city. The cardinal, however, followed the advice of Count Pier Nofri of Montedoglio, whom he had appointed head of the city guard and in whom he had great confidence. Ignoring the opinions of those who were more expert than the count, the cardinal undertook a plan of defense that took longer to complete, was less secure, and much more expensive to man than the needs and safety of the city required. (At a more opportune time I shall prove this in a separate discourse on the way to fortify Florence and other places.)

While I am describing provisions for the city's defense, however, I must note that when the Florentines were first required by the pope to join the Holy League and obligate themselves to the conditions governing it, a few were opposed. The wisest of the councillors (who were, as always, few in number) did not believe that Florence should do anything in opposition to the emperor either overtly or in secret, since the city was in no condition to bear great expense, and since it was not the custom of our city to undertake such grandiose projects. They believed that even if the League were victorious, Florence stood to gain nothing, but were they to lose, it would be her ruin. Furthermore, they argued, if the pope insisted on their participation in the League, it was absolutely necessary that their adherence be undeclared. It was even more crucial to come to terms with His Holiness on the sum of money that was to be disbursed each month. Under no circumstances should Florence put her financial outlays either at the discretion of the pope or on the basis of the cost of the war. These councillors feared that the war would be difficult and prolonged, and they recalled the example of the campaign undertaken in '21 by Pope Leo X against the French. The fact that the expense of that war had been unbearable and subject to no limitation seemed to them cause for even greater concern in the current crisis, since now they were to fight a more successful and more powerful enemy, while Florence found herself much lower in funds than before.

But the others of the Council, who were in the majority, were eager to comply with the pope's wishes. Without considering the consequences of so serious an action, nor how much harm it could cause to the pope and to our city, they publicly urged agreement to the pontiff's plans. And so, as usual, the majority pulled the minority along with them, and together they adopted the resolution that was most destructive to our city.

No one should be surprised at this, since long experience has shown that the more people there are in a council, the worse their decisions turn out. This results either from conflicting natures among the councillors, or from the inordinate love everyone has for his own opinion, or because of the emulation – not to say (speaking frankly) envy – that springs up among them. Many people are convinced, of course, that when there is a diversity of natures and opinions among councillors, as is most often the case, a sounder policy will result. They argue that the more a good proposal is challenged, the more it will prevail, like gold being separated from dross in the refiner's fire. Similarly the best proposal is supposed to shine more plainly and brightly, before those who seek it dispassionately and recognize it when it is uncovered. I maintain, however, that one wise man with authority and the people's confidence should be listened to, and his advice followed, and then it cannot happen, as it generally does now, that the worst advice wins out in debate.

It is also important that the decision-maker be exceptionally prudent, or at least have sufficient ability and judgment to recognize which advice is the best. People are always saying that this or that prince (because of his age or nature, say) was not as wise or capable of governing as he should have been, but because he had capable men around him who advised him, he acted with great prudence. But if he didn't know how to choose the best proposal from among different opinions, he would always be confused and his actions inconsistent, unless by chance he happened to pay attention to just one of them who also happened to be wiser than the others.

The more prudent a prince is, the more willing he should be to hear the opinions of those who continually observe and consider the patterns of human action. Nature rarely gives a single person all the attributes the perfect adviser needs. One will be even-tempered, another will excel in ingenuity and memory, some will be eloquent, while others who don't speak well understand how to solve problems. From among a chosen group of four or six, a body is composed in which all the factors that produce the best advice are united, and with them a prudent prince cannot err; but when this number, or a larger one, come together without a head or a wise director, it is ineffectual, for the reasons noted above. Then whoever is most charming, or most like his hearers, who supports the unreasonable wishes of the prince or the people with more eloquence or more audacity than anyone else, easily persuades the majority to his opinion. And for these reasons, it very rarely happens (as in this instance) that the best advice prevails.

For this reason alone, the ancient Romans, who governed themselves very soundly for many centuries, always appointed a dictator during the greatest and most serious crises that their republic faced; and they committed their fortunes and those of their country entirely to his will and prudence. And even though in their day there was no lack of excellent leaders, capable of freeing their city from any serious threat, nonetheless, these wise patricians, knowing by experience how important for the general safety the swift choice of the best option was (which for the reasons narrated above does not come from the majority), in emergencies voluntarily submitted themselves to the rule of a single man.

Returning to my story, however: at this point our city found itself more exposed to attack by the imperial forces than any of the other allies. Having spent not only an unbearable but an unbelievable amount of money to pay for the ill-conceived plans of those who were continually at the ears of Clement VII, the city was in a very low state of morale. And even though the cardinal of Cortona continued to fortify the city (as I said) in various places, everyone was in a state of great fear and apprehension. The pontiff meanwhile was discussing peace terms with the agents of Caesar, as he had often done in the past. It may be that as universal pastor he wanted to show His Majesty that he was fulfilling his duty to make peace among Christian princes and to reunite them so that they could resist and oppose the forces of the infidels more effectively. Or it may be that he had finally realized how little he could rely on the forces of the League or base his hopes on the promises and practices of the duke of Urbino and the French; or he may have wished to show his willingness to respond in some way to the wishes and fears of the Florentines, and that minority in particular who had opposed obligating the city to such a dangerous policy. His Holiness, however, carried on with the war cold-bloodedly, neither concluding an agreement nor breaking off negotiations.

Consequently, the peace talks had no other effect than to increase the determination of the enemy, to diminish the pope's standing among his allies, and to nourish his own vain hopes by convincing him that he could reach an agreement whenever he wanted to. The government of France complained repeatedly to its ambassadors about these talks, and the Venetian and French ambassadors frequently voiced complaints against them in Rome in the presence of His Holiness. The pope nonetheless assured all the allies that he was undertaking these talks with the enemy for their common benefit and not because he intended to break with the League. He asserted that he understood clearly what Caesar's intentions towards the Church and towards Italy were, and how great were the thirst and ambition of his agents.

While this state of indecision persisted among the allies, the Venetians decided to send Marco Foscari, one of their leading noblemen, as ambassador to Florence. By his presence and through the promises of the Republic of Venice, he was to win over those who were more inclined towards negotiation than war. In order to demonstrate the same inclination of mind, the Florentines sent their ambassador Alessandro de' Pazzi, a well educated and quick-witted young man, to Venice charging him that in addition to offering whatever the Venetians desired, he was to urge the doge and the other senators to order the duke of Urbino into Tuscany and encourage him to engage the enemy.

At about this time, the viceroy of Naples, once he had united the forces of the realm with those that had been brought over by sea, attacked Frosinone. This is a fortified town of the Church in Campania, about thirty miles from Rome. Two thousand men of the Black Bands, who had been fighting under Signor Giovanni, suddenly and unexpectedly found themselves under siege there. Although these men had very little food and lacked many other things necessary to their defense, they were nonetheless determined to defend the town. Fearlessly and with surprising ease, they repulsed several assaults against them, even after the imperial army had beaten down a large portion of the town walls with their artillery.

At this point the pope sent Vitello Vitelli with a large army of Italian soldiers and cavalry plus two thousand Swiss to relieve them. Cardinal Trivulzio from Milan, who happened to be legate to this army, accompanied them. Not only did these troops dislodge the viceroy from his position and thus liberate those who were besieged, but in one engagement their infantry destroyed a good number of the Germans who had recently arrived in Italy. They caused panic in the rest of the army, and if they had quickly followed up their victory as they should have, they would have turned and routed the entire army. That would have caused an enormous change in the kingdom of Naples. Either they didn't recognize their opportunity, or their leaders were too timid by nature, and so they halted with the intention (as they affirmed) of attacking the imperial camp on the following day. Recognizing the danger they were in, the viceroy retreated with his forces secretly that same night and quickly marched to Ceprano, a very strong fortress on the river Liri, where they could not easily be dislodged. And in order to keep the enemy occupied after they had become aware of the retreat, the imperial forces left most of their baggage and two pieces of heavy artillery behind. Still disengaged from the enemy and camped at Ponte Castello, situated on a hill, the Legate Trivulzio afterwards made an effort to keep the imperial forces at Ceprano from being supplied.

A few days earlier, Renzo da Ceri had taken Aquila with the cooperation of the Guelf faction. Displaying the ferocity that is generally practiced against an enemy party, he avenged the injuries and offenses of the past with extreme cruelty and effected great changes in the poor castles and villages of the Abruzzi. Neither Captain Doria with his armada, nor Orazio Baglioni, who had recently been released from prison by the pope, diminished their intense harassment of the ports near Naples. The latter had already taken Salerno, and the former was at Gaeta with a large number of soldiers.

Surrounded by forces whose power and menace were increasing every day, the viceroy was in a dangerous position. At the same time, he knew that his own forces were very demoralized and that the Guelf faction was creating disturbances throughout the kingdom of Naples. In consequence, he began to moderate the conditions of an agreement that had been under discussion for some time with the pontiff through the intermediacy of the general of the Franciscan Order. This was Friar Francesco degli Angeli, a close relative of Caesar's, who had been sent several months beforehand into Italy by His Imperial Majesty for this purpose. Finally, after many revisions, the conditions seemed tolerable to His Holiness and those who advised him. Since His Holiness, by his own account, was without money and extremely short on supplies, he concluded an agreement with the viceroy in March of '27, without including his allies or even giving them notice beforehand. The terms were these:

§ All imperial armies and forces, including the lancers recently arrived in Italy, were to retreat and return to the positions they occupied before the war started.

§ The Castello and city of Milan were to be restored to Francesco Sforza as legitimate duke, along with the rest of his former duchy.

§ The kingdom of Naples would remain in the free possession of the emperor; and he was to relocate all his soldiers there.

§ The Germans, after receiving three wage allocations from His Holiness, would immediately return to their own country.

§ Both sides were vigorously to pursue war against the infidel at common expense.

§ The allies were to be allowed three months time in which to ratify the agreement if they wished.

When the allies learned of this agreement, it was disapproved by all of them but condemned for different reasons by different groups. The cardinals and the prelates were against it because they were convinced that victory had been certain and because they felt their pomp and grandeur would be diminished by it. The French and the English opposed it because they were afraid, since they had not been involved in the negotiations and since the pope was inclined and obligated to Caesar's will, that the emperor would have little need to take either king into account in the future. The Venetians disliked it because they felt that it would quickly shift the theater of war into their territory. The government of Florence distrusted the agreement, even though large numbers of its citizens had previously urged it on the pope, because, having delayed so long, they were fearful of the viceroy's duplicity. They were especially fearful of Bourbon, who was far advanced in the field and in command of a very substantial force, to whom he had repeatedly promised the opportunity of sacking Tuscany. Bourbon had not participated in drafting the treaty and was unlikely to ratify it since he lost his claim to Milan because of it. On his account all the allies of His Holiness were extremely ill at ease.

These diverse assessments by the allies added up to a uniform condemnation of the accord that had been made without their consent. Drawn on by his own misguided thinking and by his pitiable and wretched fate into a path that was entirely inimical to his welfare and that of the whole of luckless Italy, the pontiff agreed to it. He signed it without bothering to learn the opinions of his allies or whether Bourbon was likely to violate it. He pleaded that he had capitulated under duress, first because of his extreme lack of funds and supplies, and secondly because of the delays and strange actions of the duke of Urbino and the procrastination of the French. In addition to these reasons, he insisted that the mind and will of Caesar were intent on universal peace, which he believed he would guarantee by signing the accord.

Despite what many believe, this error of judgment would not have destroyed the pope, if he had not compounded it afterwards with another one that was more glaring and much more serious. Trusting too much to the agreement that had been reached and urged on by his extreme avarice, he very soon discharged the two thousand Swiss and those soldiers of the Black Bands at Frosinone. Without question he should have retained them until he was certain of Bourbon's intentions and those of his army and knew that the terms of the agreement were being adhered to by those who had already arrogated the best of Italy to themselves.

While the affairs of the kingdom of Naples were in the turmoil described above, and negotiations were still going on in Rome, Monseigneur de Bourbon continued his unsuccessful efforts to pry his Spaniards out of Milan and unite them with the German lancers. Until they were merged, the forces could not come to the aid of the viceroy. At last he was forced to give the Spaniards two additional pay allotments, which he extracted with considerable difficulty from the nobles and people of Milan.

Finally, leaving half of them behind in Milan under the command of Antonio de Leva, he led the rest to a position near the German lancers along the banks of the Po, but on the Lombard (northern) side of the river. And even though the Spaniards and Germans from Milan were still very reluctant to join up with the Lutherans newly arrived from Germany for the reasons stated above, nonetheless, after still further negotiation, he got them to cross the Po. After repeatedly promising them the opportunity to sack both Florence and Rome, he succeeded in marching his united force towards Piacenza.

This army gave no indication of the route they were planning to take or whether they intended to attack any of the towns and cities of the Church along the way. Having passed Piacenza and turned towards Modena, they bypassed the road for Pontrémoli (as there was no doubt in the minds of many that they would do) since it was a longer, steeper, and poorer road, and lacked the infinite other advantages that were to be found along the road to Bologna. Still there was no reason to fear that they would attack Piacenza or Parma – both cities belonging to the Church – since they were well supplied and heavily defended, and the imperial forces lacked sufficient artillery and munitions for use in the field, let alone against cities.

Once the imperial troops had passed Piacenza, the lieutenant-general and the marquis of Saluzzo with their troops and some others quickly moved on to Bologna. They left Parma well garrisoned, and they had Count Guido Rangoni with many arquebusiers and cavalry move to defend Modena. From Bologna the lieutenant-general and the other officers tried to figure out Bourbon's intentions. Attacking no towns and scarcely doing battle, he was nonetheless consuming and destroying everything in the rural areas that he passed through. With twenty thousand seasoned troops, fierce and ready for battle, he arrived at S. Giovanni in Persiceto, ten miles from Bologna. Meanwhile the duke of Urbino, who was still commanding the Venetian forces, slowly approached the Po, even though he was repeatedly begged by the agents of the League to march with all possible speed to Bologna. He declared that he did not wish to cross the river before he had seen the enemy take the road for Tuscany and Romagna. He said he was afraid that they might turn into the Polesine region and attack the Venetian state from that direction with support from the duke of Ferrara.

Now Francesco Maria had indicated at various times to some of his friends that he wanted above everything else for San Leo and the rest of the territory of Montefeltro to be returned to him. If the Florentines and His Holiness would not oblige him, he declared that he would abandon them in their greatest difficulty. This news soon came to the ears of the lieutenant-general. He knew how Francesco Maria avoided danger on any pretext, and how necessary it was that he cross the Apennines (as he had frequently promised) as soon as Bourbon showed his intention of moving into Tuscany. He also knew how little the Florentines valued the possession of San Leo, and so he easily reached an agreement with the duke for the return of all the territory of Montefeltro. For his part, Francesco Maria promised to cross the Apennines when Bourbon got close to Bologna. This arrangement was readily accepted by those who managed the government in Florence without His Holiness being informed. Afterwards, however, the pope made it very clear that he would not have consented. This was either because of his great hatred of the duke, or because he preferred that the war and its dangers be confined to Tuscany; or it may be that he was angry because he hadn't been consulted beforehand.

Whatever his reason, I don't want to postpone any longer describing the pope's efforts to reach agreement with the duke of Ferrara at the time when the twelve thousand German lancers had first arrived in the territory of Mantua. His Holiness offered terms that should certainly have proved persuasive to the duke; and while he still appeared to be considering them, the lieutenant-general, who was handling the negotiations (and felt they were nearing a successful conclusion), situated himself a few miles from Ferrara. At this point, the duke informed him that he would not proceed further with the negotiations, since on the preceding day he had received the text of an agreement with Caesar from the Spanish ambassador. Through this agreement everything he had lost was to be reinstated. The terms were such that he neither could nor would fail to confirm them, especially since he was a relative of Caesar's. Hearing this, the lieutenant-general returned immediately with little honor to Parma.

This example, like the many other similar ones narrated above, demonstrates how the plans of princes conceived in evil fortune fail when they come to be carried out, and what damage their failures cause. If the pope had offered not even the same terms but somewhat less to the duke of Ferrara at the beginning of the war, as he should have, without doubt the duke would have accepted. Being wise the duke would have settled for much less rather than be separated from the other Italian states and alienated from France. But because of Clement's obstinacy and the ambitions of the administrators of the Church territories, the duke came out against the pope at the very time when the Church and the League needed him most. And so during the entire time that the imperial army remained at S. Giovanni in Persiceto, they were supported with money and provisions from Ferrara, in addition to the aid which the Ferrarese had given in secret at the beginning of the march of the lancers into Italy. The whole time they remained at S. Giovanni in Persiceto, they endured continuous rain and snow, which were very heavy, despite the lateness of the season. Consequently they suffered from lack of shelter, and their food supplies were uncertain. If they had not been aided from Ferrara, they would not have lasted two days. In this and many other ways the duke supported and advised Bourbon. He also encouraged and supported the Florentine exiles who were in Ferrara.

While Bourbon and his army were seeing to their supplies and other necessities for their thrust into Tuscany by the road through Bologna and Sasso Marconi, the Spanish soldiers of the united force mutinied against Bourbon, since they had not received as much money as the Germans had. Their uprising was so sudden and violent that if Bourbon had not taken refuge in the camp of the German lancers, without doubt the Spaniards would have killed him. Later on, however, after they had all been reconciled and were again ready to move out, Captain George von Frundsberg was seized by an apoplexy and a catarrh of such seriousness that he was carried to Ferrara on the point of death. These unforeseen events, happening one after the other in this way, kept the army in place some days longer than those who led it intended. Finally, however, when they were newly supplied and all their difficulties seemed to have been overcome, they decided to move out the following day. They planned to take the Barberino road into the Mugello region north of Florence, and then to turn wherever opportunity beckoned. Once again they were held back, this time by an incredible snowfall. It fell all night not only on the Apennines, but it also fell in the plains they were to pass through, thickly covering them. This snowstorm was followed by such violent rainstorms that the imperial troops were again prevented from leaving S. Giovanni in Persiceto, and while they remained, they were forced to use up a large part of the provisions they had set aside for their march.

In view of the setbacks suffered by the imperial army, the lieutenant-general had sent part of his infantry to Pianoro. He had arranged the rest so that as soon as the imperials took the road for Sasso Marconi, these troops would march to Florence ahead of the enemy, where he, along with the marquis of Saluzzo and other officers with a large number of infantry and cavalry, would have preceded them.

He had reassured everyone in the city with his many letters and urged them not to fear that Florence would be attacked and taken. Nonetheless those who advised the rulers of Florence at that time were very apprehensive, though fearing less for the city than for the surrounding towns and villages. They could see no way to save them from being razed, which, even if the city were spared, would still cause its ultimate ruin. They were also concerned because they knew that many citizens, and not just commoners, were desperate and willing to risk invasion rather than be governed by Clement.

While Bourbon was waiting at S. Giovanni in Persiceto for a chance to move his troops, from a messenger of the viceroy called Fieramosca he learned of the treaty that had been concluded at Rome. After describing the agreement Caesar had made and the conditions that forced him to come to terms with the pope, Fièramosca urged and begged Bourbon to retreat with all his army beyond the Po, since this was what had been agreed to in the treaty both by the viceroy and by other agents of Caesar sent into Italy for this purpose.

Bourbon was seriously affected by this unexpected message, but he managed to conceal his anger and to express delight and approval of what the viceroy had concluded on His Majesty's orders. He promised that he would work in every way to assure that the accord made at Rome was obeyed by his entire army. At the same time, he secretly advised his Spanish and German captains that they should refuse to return to Lombardy or else the chance to sack Rome and Florence would surely slip from their grasp. In keeping with his plan, he told Fieramosca that he was afraid that his army would not agree without being given all the back pay that was owed them; but that they might agree if they were given double the sum of money that was specified in the treaty, and if it were immediately paid out to them. Otherwise, he declared, he wouldn't be able to manage them.

Bourbon advanced these and many other arguments as a means to beguile both the pope and the agents of Caesar with false hopes. In fact, His Excellency had no other intention than to lead his army, as he had promised them many times, to Florence and Rome. To avoid any appearance of disagreement with Caesar's decision, however, he put the blame on the army. Its leaders, both because of their own inclinations and also because they were advised by him, declared that unless they were given all the back pay they were owed starting from the time they left Germany to come into Italy, with the addition of various bonuses to be given to the officers, they would not comply with the terms that had been negotiated in Rome without their participation.

When the viceroy heard about these objections, he left Rome and went directly to Florence so that he could respond directly and quickly to Bourbon's demands and those of the other officers. For the sake of his honor he wanted what had been agreed on to be observed. After having sent his negotiators many times to the army, and after a great deal of argument, he concluded a second agreement with one of Bourbon's officers who had come to Florence. This agreement stipulated that within six days Bourbon's men were to be paid 100,000 scudi more than they were promised in the first agreement; the other conditions remained the same.

Our city was obligated to come up with this sum of money. Both the cash and the credit of our citizens were wearing thin, and in the current political situation it was too dangerous to use force, so in order to raise money fast it was necessary to melt down the vases and other objects of silver that were in the Palazzo della Signoria and in the richest churches and convents of Florence. Even though this appeared impious and profane to many people, those that advised it declared that in an emergency such an action was not a violation of human or divine law. Indeed both laws not only recognized the possibility but explicitly charged the governors of cities and principalities to make use of the images, vases, and other ornaments of silver and gold dedicated to the divine service. This must always be done with the intention, however, of restoring in better times objects of the same beauty and value to the same places.

While they were waiting in Florence for this sum of money to be collected, Monseigneur de Bourbon moved his army. He explained that because the Florentines were taking so long to come up with the money, his officers suspected that they were being tricked, and so they were beginning to mutiny. He left S. Giovanni in Persiceto; and since he was prevented by the heavy snow and rain from taking either the road to Bologna or the Sasso road (as he had planned), he took the Romagna road. The Germans took the major road, and the Spanish the lower road nearer the Po. They met little resistance. Nonetheless both armies pillaged and burned every house and village they encountered, without, however, attacking the fortresses or cities they passed.

After a few days they came to Cotignola, a fortified town belonging to the Church. The people of this town at first acted tough, and in fact they had several times refused forces that had been sent to help them by the officers of the Church and the League. Nonetheless, when they finally confronted the enemy face to face, they immediately negotiated a surrender (the custom of the proud and fearful). But the army did not respect the agreement and immediately sacked the town. They found it very well stocked with supplies, and so they stayed there for a few days to refresh themselves. Bourbon meanwhile kept hidden the road he intended to take, but the general opinion was that he would either go through the Marecchia into Tuscany or lead his men to Rome by way of the road through the Marches.

His Excellency remained undecided which road to take, in part because he knew that even before he had left S. Giovanni in Persiceto, officers of the League had left Bologna at night with large numbers of troops that were to be distributed through all the cities in Romagna. He also knew that the agents of the pope with considerable industry and diligence had finally overcome the objections which, despite the manifest peril of our city, French officers and the duke of Urbino had raised against the accord recently made in Florence. With their disagreements settled, things were arranged in such a way that in the shortest possible time their men could push through the valley of the Montone River or of Lamona and arrive in Florence before the enemy. Bourbon also knew that Francesco Maria was approaching Bologna, although slowly, ready to move whenever necessary into Tuscany on the Sasso road. In addition to these things, he knew that the viceroy was coming in person to look for him.

Nonetheless, when the moment seemed right to him, he marched his army at maximum speed to Méldola. Indeed, in order to move even faster, he left three pieces of heavy artillery behind at Cotignola. Méldola is a fortress near Forlì belonging to Signor Alberto da Carpi. Bourbon and his men accepted its surrender, then burned it. They then marched to Civitella, a small and weakly fortified town of the Church. He sacked this town, too, after it surrendered. He then continued his march through the valley, and with equal ferocity and cruelty he

took Galeata, Pianetto, Santa Sofia, and S. Piero in
Bagno, very weak and very small towns and villages belonging to Florence, which he burned and pillaged. Then,
having arrived at Pieve di S. Stefano where some of his
men skirmished with the defenders, but without success,
he descended into the plain by way of Anghiara and
Arezzo.

On the twenty-second of April, 1527 he arrived at
Montevarchi, where he remained for a while with his
entire army. They were completely worn out from enduring weeks of incredible shortages of supplies. For many
days the majority of the army had lived on nothing but
grasses and any sort of meat they could find, including
donkey, without tasting either bread or wine. This is not
really surprising considering the difficulty and sterility of
the long road they had taken and the poverty of the
inhabitants they had despoiled.

At the time when the imperials were moving away
from the Po, the cardinal of Cortona (without speaking
to those who customarily advised on the important affairs
of the city) commanded the Eight *(Otto di Balia)* to seize
three citizens of noble family in broad daylight outside
their houses. He did not propose interrogating them to
discover what was in the minds of the citizens. His aim
was to intimidate by example those who might be ill-
disposed towards the state. This caused the whole population great distress and anger, and it was so offensive to
some who had high positions in the government that
they went immediately to the cardinal and complained
vigorously. They argued very forcefully that it was an
extremely grave error to use such violent means when an
enemy army was approaching Florence. It was likely to
frighten many people into exile, who, because they
despaired of their safety, would try to persuade Bourbon
to march on Florence, arguing that the people were very
favorable to him. To these complaints (as was his custom)
Cortona, who was by nature a hard man, made no other

reply than that this was the pope's idea; and that those who condemned it were inferring that the pope was malicious and unwise.

This is the sort of response that is invariably given by someone who subjugates others by violence. He who holds the government in his hands never wants or admits that he needs advice, except in cases where he thinks things will be argued the way he wants them to be; and if he sometimes seems willing to listen to the opinions of those who deserve esteem, he does it either for appearances or in order to bring them little by little into compromising situations until they finally discover that their safety is bound up with his. After these three were taken prisoner, some nobles out of fear secretly fled to Ferrara, while others went to Rome to speak with the pope. Every day it was feared that others would do the same. Thus the obvious growth of dissatisfaction with the government in Florence made those outside the city increasingly bold, and fired the hopes of those within who desired liberty.

After the departure of the imperial forces from Cotignola, the lieutenant-general, who was at Forlì, immediately wrote to Florence and Rome and informed them of the enemy's movements. Then having departed in haste with all the troops in Romagna, he marched with them to Florence by the road through Marradi, meanwhile encouraging the duke of Urbino to do the same. At Castrocaro, however, he found himself in company with the viceroy and convinced him to go in person to find Bourbon, who had not waited for him at Cotignola. The lieutenant-general believed that the presence of the viceroy would convince the Germans and Spaniards who were (at that time) in Galeata, that they should not advance further into Florentine territory. The viceroy set off immediately with an armed escort. Near Santa Sofia he came upon some peasants who took him for an enemy and attacked him, even though he was accompanied by representatives of the Florentine commissioners. When the viceroy saw that some of his escort were wounded and some taken prisoner, he fled. Because of the speed and surefootedness of his horse, and with the help of some other peasants, he reached the hermitage at Camáldoli. From there he communicated to Bourbon, who was now near Pieve Santo Stefano, that he wanted to meet with him. They set a meeting for the following day, and met near Vernia, where they remained a short while, then towards evening they went together to the camp of the imperial forces. When they had learned of the viceroy's arrival, the officers of the army confronted him and made very clear with words and gestures that they did not welcome him. There were some who gave every indication of wishing to harm him, but the presence of Bourbon restrained them.

These risks and hardships, quite out of keeping with his dignity, which the viceroy endured, as well as the contents of letters Bourbon wrote to Antonio de Leva, which were intercepted, proved to many that the viceroy wanted the treaty he had concluded in Rome to take effect. Others, however, were convinced that he only wanted to fool the pope. It is obvious, however, and not only from these indications, that His Excellency had methods that were surer, more cautious, and more honorable to bend His Holiness to his will, should the pope be inclined to a policy that was different from the one he espoused in words. The viceroy continued to argue with great insistence that the accord made at Rome and afterwards confirmed in Florence should be upheld. To this end, he negotiated another agreement with Bourbon before he arrived in Arezzo with his army, not very different from the earlier one, except that a much greater sum of money was to be paid out almost immediately. He also promised to have the pope's ratification of this within six days.

The viceroy, therefore, immediately wrote several letters to His Holiness which he sent by different mounted messengers, then awaited his reply at Montevarchi. Because of this agreement, the Spanish and Germans did not do as much damage in the countryside after they left Pieve S. Stefano as they had before. They sacked Laterina and Rondine, however, because they had resisted very forcefully despite their weakness, and many people there were killed.

If I had narrated the crucial events that occurred from the genesis of the holy and venerable League until the time that the imperial troops arrived in Valdarno in greater detail and with an eye to the rules of history, they would show more clearly that fortune has always been on the side of the imperials, and that delay and timidity always characterized the army of the League. Nonetheless, knowing that others more diligent than I would be writing about these events, I have left many details for them to fill in. It was not my intention to narrate all the major events that happened in my day (as many praiseworthy historians have done in their works) but only to recount the shameful sack of Rome.

My aim was to show, at least in part, the ruin and disaster that threaten states and governments which are badly advised and worse administered in their affairs. And in the following book I force myself to place in detail before the reader's eyes the rapes, murders, sacrileges, and cruelties practiced daily by the treacherous Germans and the Spanish in this sorrowful time in which I write. I do this so that everyone in the future can better understand the just wrath of God against a rich and noble city. From this story those who govern and advise republics and principalities can learn wisdom at the expense of others, because there is seldom an opportunity to profit from one's own ruin.

* *
*

BOOK TWO

INTRODUCTION

HE TERRIBLE EVENTS that have occurred from 1494 up to the present day have brought all of Italy to the brink of ruin. Their example should make not only the wise governors of republics and principalities but even the ignorant multitude realize that no organization and no preparation offers greater security than to be inside your own fortified walls protected by your own army. In our common disaster everyone recognizes the cause of our mortal wounds and of the death that seems to be waiting for us and for our homeland. Nonetheless, held back by a long-term habit of cowardice, people don't know how to prepare themselves or persuade others to follow the glorious examples of the well-constituted republics of Antiquity.

It is clear that they kept themselves secure over such a long period and attained their well-known eminence only by maintaining their civilization and worthy customs under the shadow and protection of severe military discipline. Without perfecting such discipline it is impossible to enjoy peace or acquire wealth and grandeur. But everyone in our day is confused and confounded. We look at one another like frightened sheep penned up in the slaughterhouse, expecting any moment to see our resources, our families, and our beloved homeland in the hands of barbarous and bestial nations thirsting beyond all limit for our riches and our blood. And this supreme failing of our times deserves even less excuse, the less we attempt a remedy (even though it is easy).

Consider how small a number of foreigners fearlessly range through our miserable Italy every day, assaulting cities, taking them with ease, sacking them without mercy and with little cost to themselves, then occupying them in happiness and security as long as it suits them. Certainly we should be ashamed of our cowardice and our failure to resist these armies. Nowhere in history is so much ignorance and so much neglect to be found in other nations as we have been seeing now for thirty-three years in our unfortunate Italy. Many times in the past as if drowned and submerged by a rapid torrent, Italy was overrun, sacked, devastated, and occupied by foreign hordes. In those cases, though, we read that for those barbarian nations victory and glory came bloody. Here again the example of our predecessors puts us to shame, since nowadays four, six, or twelve thousand untrained foreigners, poorly armed and lacking leadership, harass, consume, and overpower this country of ours. And in response the wise give up hope and join the ignorant in declaring that there is no way for us to head off this scourge sent by the wrath of God, and that for our horrible sins we deserve such punishment and worse.

These are the complaints and laments (according to my judgment) of those who are too downcast and entirely lacking in that nobility of spirit that is natural to humanity. After all, what experience or dogma holds us back and decrees that, even if we wished, we could not through good habits and virtuous works change the divine sentence (speaking as a Christian) that is passed in anger against us? Certainly divine goodness will incline to us whenever it sees the love of poverty and justice reborn in our hearts. It will respond, too, when we are ready and willing with our own proper and ordinary arms to defend our lives and our city with obstinacy, or to die courageously. But if the promises of some modern prophet persuade us that we are going to be helped by God and liberated by Him while we persist in effeminate and abominable vices and in laziness and pusillanimity, then we are certainly ignorant and wrong; and we await celestial help in vain. For if we don't change our ways, our sentence will not change; but each day with greater menace it will hang over our heads.

And if our own ruin has no meaning for us (as with reason it should), posterity will surely acknowledge our cowardice along with whatever benefit they may happen to derive from our example. When human affairs are forced down to the lowest rung of misery, they are incapable of further decline, and little by little, driven by necessity (the mother of virtue), they begin to ascend the scale of happiness. Through virtue they come to the final and highest rung. Those who let themselves be taken over and conquered by irresponsibility – the root cause of every disorder and the source of all destruction – don't usually stay here long. Irresponsible neglect makes everything go awry and leads society to the depths all over again.

Human beings are constantly in motion: rising and falling, they pass from good to evil, from evil to good. But where virtue and unity are best preserved and people fight their own battles, nations remain longer in a state of happiness and enjoy the grandeur they have acquired. Where irresponsibility, discord, and timidity are found, the state comes more quickly to its final extermination. Italy is more deeply mired in these vices at present than it ever was in past centuries and beset by innumerable other vices and failings that derive from these three principal disorders. Thanks for this are due not so much to secular as to ecclesiastical rulers, who have continually led and commanded here. It is no wonder that in these days Italy could be so easily overrun, beaten down, and stripped by a mere twelve thousand foreigners, nor would it be surprising if in the future they brought her to total ruin, an image not unlike the scene that will end this second book.

HUS, ON THE TWENTY-SECOND OF April in 1527 (as briefly told in the previous book), Monseigneur de Bourbon found himself in Montevarchi with an even larger army than he had had outside Bologna. The increase was made up of the many Italian soldiers who wanted to share in a notable victory and sack. They had joined up with these foreigners in various places (as is the custom of our wrong-headed soldiers), despite the difficulties of supply, and the march, and the lack of pay, and indifferent to the fact that they were joining the common enemy in the final destruction of Italy. This is certainly miserable behavior, and at the end of the war it warrants severe reprisals against those who fought on the side of the foreigners by every prince and republic. The imperial army welcomed them, knowing that their presence weakened the enemy and made their army more formidable.

As long as the imperial forces remained in Florentine territory, the pope refused to ratify an amended agreement. He had responded repeatedly to the viceroy's messages by insisting that he did not wish to discuss any conventions whatsoever until the enemy army returned to where it had been when the accord was first agreed on in Rome. Discontented and having suffered great damage to his reputation, the viceroy returned to Siena. His Holiness' response was not based on the treachery of Bourbon, of which he was unaware, but on his conviction that the difficulties that the imperial army were currently experiencing would force them in a short time to ask for an agreement under more favorable terms.

This hope of His Holiness was further reinforced by the fact that almost all the forces of the League were gathered near Florence and his belief that our city could and would easily repulse any attack because of its strong fortifications. He clung to his belief despite his knowledge that the entire population despised him and ma-

ligned his government and his agents without restraint.
He also knew that many people, including the rich and
noble, were desperate and would not resist in case of an
attack. In fact they were willing to have the Germans capture and sack Florence (even though this was dangerous
and shameful), believing that this was the only way they
could liberate themselves from enslavement to the papal
government. Despair of this kind is neither beneficial nor
praiseworthy; and there were many more honorable ways
for the city to escape from Clement's hands at a more
appropriate time. But the greater such despair is, the
more it must be taken into account by those who rule
imperiously over people who are accustomed to live in
liberty. This is especially true when many nobles, who had
great resources, would rather see themselves the victims of
such cruel enemies than continue to endure government
by force and against their will.

His Holiness imagined that in a situation as perilous
as this, the majority of noble and wealthy Florentines
would keep those who supported the Lutherans in check.
He felt that most of the people would cooperate fully in
the defense and preservation of their own wealth, their
children, and their fatherland. In order to quiet the fear
among the citizens of Florence that they would be forced
to pay as much money in the present crisis as they had
paid up to that point with such unwillingness and difficulty, the pope declared that within a few days he would
create several cardinals for large sums of money.

But just as the other plans for this campaign turned
out badly for His Blessedness, this one also went awry.
There were various prelates and others who had given
firm indications in the past that they were ready to pay
40,000 or 50,000 scudi each whenever cardinals were to be
created. Because the Church was in danger and merchants were unable to raise such large sums of money
quickly in the present crisis, these men failed him. And
this is what happens when you wait till the last minute to

make necessary provisions, those, I say, which can and must be made much sooner.

In Florence the majority of the young nobles were very eager for the cardinal of Cortona to issue arms to each citizen. He had indicated to them several times that he intended to do this, and he had recently ordered that the number of men in Florence between the ages of sixteen and forty be determined. At last, the young men realized that they were being put off, and in order to obtain arms more quickly and more surely, the majority of the most noble of them spoke many times to the *gonfaloniere* for justice who was serving at that time. They knew that he was a strong supporter of arming the citizens. He believed that among other benefits, this would allow the city to be defended with greater security and at less expense. A mixed force of mercenaries and its own well-organized citizens would be stronger and cheaper than a force made up only of mercenaries.

Knowing that the youth were determined to be armed, and that they would not hesitate to take arms by force, the *gonfaloniere* on the twenty-sixth of April in '27 finally obtained permission from the cardinal to distribute arms to everyone. With the agreement of the cardinal and of the Signoria, he had already arranged with the *gonfalonieri* of companies that they would each assemble their men in the most suitable churches, and once they were armed would march them, without creating disturbance, to the Piazza della Signoria. There the organization and the commander of each company would be appointed, and the role that each company was to play in the defense of the city would be announced.

And while the *gonfalonieri* were carrying out their duties in the various churches, at 2:00 PM near the Mercato Nuovo, Rinaldo Corsini began to speak out against those who then ruled the city and to advocate its liberation from slavery to the Medici. The young men who had first insisted on having arms imagined that a popular uprising was beginning. They assumed that since the majority had the same reasons as they did to oppose the government, they were also of equal courage and determination. They concluded that the people would quickly respond to Corsini's appeal and take up arms against the government. They were convinced (as was indeed credible) that the uprising had greater support than it afterwards turned out to have. Without organization and without reliable intelligence, after arming very quickly, they ran to the Palazzo della Signoria. Recognizing the danger that threatened the city, some of the senators who governed with the cardinal had entered the palazzo shortly before this. They knew that the cardinal of Cortona and Signor Ippolito had left the city to meet the duke of Urbino, who was coming to Florence that evening to consult on very important matters.

Finding the palazzo poorly guarded, the young men had entered it. Yet even after it had been in their control for several hours, they failed to do anything to seize control of the government. They made no effort to consult with the middle-aged and older citizens, who had assembled at the palazzo when they heard the noise of the uprising. Together they might consider what was to follow and undertake such actions as barring the gates of the city, taking command of the artillery, and driving out of the Medici palazzo anyone who had any part in the government. It would have been a good idea, too, to run through all the streets and call on everyone in the name of "Liberty and the People!" All these are acts very necessary in such movements. But they neglected all of these things and did nothing but have the bell sounded. They imagined that at the sound of the bell all the people would eagerly take up arms as they had at other times.

But the whole population did not come running armed to the Palazzo della Signoria as it should have. And as a result, the young men simply wasted their time while the palazzo was in their control, and they let a longed-for opportunity escape from their hands. For if the Porta San Gallo had been barred when the duke of Urbino reached it, and if he had then heard that the people refused to obey the pope any longer, there is no doubt that he would not have attempted to force the gates. He himself affirmed this afterwards many times, and it would have been in keeping with his great hatred for the Medici.

After the noblemen, who reached the palazzo first, many other men of lower rank ran there, and among them there were men more mature in age but angrier and less restrained than they should have been. With the palazzo under the control of the people and full of armed men who were swollen with hatred against the Medici, the supreme magistrate was forced to do whatever these men wanted. Some of them for no apparent reason wounded two of the senators. And afterwards Jacopo Alamanni in a wicked and furious rage stabbed the *gonfaloniere* with a very sharp dagger in the back and the neck (although ineffectively), while he was sitting with his companions in the public audience hall. This very same Alamanni had been held at baptism by the *gonfaloniere* for justice, and was often helped by him; nonetheless, he stabbed the magistrate.

Because of this attack, word spread immediately through the palazzo and the city that the *gonfaloniere* had been killed. This seemed more plausible since somewhat earlier many of his clothes had been thrown into the piazza from the windows of his apartments. These chaotic and violent events and many others like them overwhelmed those who would have responded more effectively to this opportunity. The state of extreme confusion and tumultuous disorder stymied everyone and prevented more prudent measures from being taken.

I could also describe in detail how the *gonfaloniere* for justice (being more in possession of himself than it appeared to the others in the palazzo) always maintained the dignity of his position despite the confused and dangerous situation. He comforted, advised, restrained, encouraged, or disciplined men as their character and emotional state required. I am aware, however, of how reprehensible it is, without very necessary reasons, to write of oneself; therefore I will leave these subjects to others who will write this history in more detail.

While this tumult was continuing in the city, the cardinal of Cortona, Cardinals Cibo and Ridolfi, and Signor Ippolito were all absent, having gone (as I noted above) to meet the duke of Urbino. The duke was coming to Florence that day to discuss where, given the proximity of the lancers, the army of the League was to make camp near the city. From several messengers dispatched by those who were then in the Medici Palazzo, Cortona learned that the Palazzo della Signoria had been taken over and that a large part of the population were rising up against the government. He sent orders that certain captains of the guard quickly, and without revealing their intention, were to take the Faenza gate with whatever forces they could muster. He commanded others to go as quickly as possible to the Medici Palazzo and assemble their troops there and position them in such a way that the palazzo could not be forced by the people.

The cardinal of Cortona himself soon arrived in the city together with the other cardinals, the duke of Urbino, an adequate number of soldiers, and some small cannon. Without delay, they all moved quickly towards the palazzo. They reached Orsanmichele easily, without being opposed at all by those who had been declaring (as is the common custom) that they loved liberty more than their own lives. From some of the officers of the infantry companies that were already spread out in the piazza they learned that the young men inside were firing steadily and that their shots had already killed some of the men. Before attempting to take the palazzo by force, they thought it would be more prudent to sound out the intentions and the resolve of those inside.

They sent Signor Federigo da Bozzoli into the palazzo, not only to find out the intentions of the men inside but also to observe the situation there and to determine whether they were in a position to resist if they decided not to leave voluntarily. He found those within very intent on maintaining their liberty and persevering in what they had started. Realizing, therefore, that his mission could bear no fruit, and that he could not persuade those under arms in the palazzo to surrender it to Signor Ippolito voluntarily (even though he had offered unconditional pardon to everyone), he headed back to tell the cardinal that he had failed to negotiate an agreement. He intended to describe what he had seen and heard inside and to show the cardinal how the palazzo could be taken without much difficulty.

Before he had regained Orsanmichele, however, he encountered Francesco Guicciardini. The lieutentant-general had gone to meet him on purpose, in hopes that with the help of Signor Federigo he might avert the terrible catastrophe that threatened the city that day. The lieutenant-general had few options, since he knew the cardinal was ready to use force once he concluded that he could not regain the palazzo by surrender. He also knew that Francesco Maria had sent in haste for his infantry, who were encamped near the walls of the city. His Excellency had told Cortona in his presence that he didn't want to wait till the evening to attack, because when the people were fearful, it was very easy to overcome them. His purpose was to give the people time after the assault on the palazzo to regain courage and to come together so that if Bourbon attacked later they would aggressively defend the city.

Knowing all this, Messer Francesco had waited for Signor Federigo. When he had spoken with him outside the palazzo, he learned that those within were determined to defend it and that His Lordship judged that it would be easy to take it by storm. He immediately began to urge Signor Federigo with all his eloquence not to be the cause of a great disaster, but to save the palazzo and the city both. He argued that in such cases violence does not end where people intend it to, but fear or desperation forces events into directions entirely different from those the ostensible victor foresees. Because he was a very close friend, and because Signor Federigo wanted to do what Guicciardini had convinced him the pope would prefer – that is to regain the palazzo with clemency rather than overcome it with violence – the lieutenant-general was able to convince him to follow his plan.

And so Signor Federigo described the situation to the cardinal in milder terms than he had found it, and said that only the fear of being punished had induced those within to refuse to surrender. On the other hand, he argued that there would be great difficulty in taking the palazzo by force, because of its strength and the number of its defenders; and because it was to be feared that when the fighting began the men inside would be aided by the whole population, especially since night was coming on. These arguments convinced Cortona to send Signor Federigo once more into the palazzo, this time accompanied by Messer Francesco, with generous offers of pardon for everyone (even though many were against the idea). These two, along with his brother the *gonfaloniere*, and in the presence of the senators, took pains to convince the leaders of the uprising of the great danger they would face if they did not come to an agreement. They argued that no hope could be placed in the people, who had abandoned them when they were unopposed; and now that the city was full of the duke of Urbino's men, they were much less likely to come to the aid of those in the palazzo. Should they voluntarily surrender the palazzo to the Medici, however, they would be taking a course that guaranteed everyone would be safe and secure. And so, after much argument, they finally decided to leave the building and agreed to leave it in the condition they found it when they had first taken it, providing the agreement was drawn up in such a way that they could rely on it.

At this point, recognizing that everyone was in agreement, they sent to Orsanmichele for the surrender document that had been signed by Cardinal Cortona, Cardinal Cibo, and Signor Ippolito, and afterwards by the duke (even though he put his hand to it with reluctance, arguing that he could not promise it would be observed by those who were not under his command). It was also signed by the marquis of Saluzzo and the Venetian quartermaster-general. When it had been delivered to the *gonfaloniere* and found to be satisfactory to everyone, the young men and the others in arms who had been inside returned sadly to their houses.

It was wise of both parties to accept this agreement. If the government had retaken the palazzo by force and killed a number of those inside, the Medici would have been hated more and therefore been in even greater danger from the rest of the city than they had been before. Because of the proximity of the lancers, this was not to be taken lightly. If Bourbon had found out that the people and the Medici were fighting each other, he would immediately have advanced on the city, either on his own, invited by exiles, or appealed to by the people. He could assume that he would be favored and helped to enter the city by some group inside. People would rather be conquered by an enemy than be overcome by their own soldiers; for hatred of one's own is a much stronger force than fear of the enemy.

As for the youth who were in the palazzo – under siege with few arms and fewer food supplies and unsupported by the people – they would have been very wrong not to consent to the accord, especially since their deaths would have precipitated the destruction of their country.

They could still hope that one day on a better, safer, and more laudable occasion they might see Florence liberated, once it was saved from the present danger. By submitting it to the violence and rapacity of enemy occupation, they would have been forcing it into a longer and more cruel subjugation.

After the youth had left the palazzo, as I have said, the Medici retook it and stationed large garrisons of guards in various locations within it and in the city generally, especially in their houses and in the Piazza della Signoria. These guards were continually vigilant (more so at night than during the day) as if they were expecting at any moment to have to fight against the people. But the people, who had repented too late of their failure to take up arms when they were called by the bell, now saw their enemy grow more numerous every hour inside the city, while large numbers of foreigners spread throughout their territory. Fearing the one no less than the other, they were all confused and desperate. In consequence, many of those who had taken part in the seizure of the palazzo and many others who had made no move at all, seeing danger on every hand, fled for their safety; some to Lucca and some further. This exodus was intensified by the agents and servants of the Medici who were saying things calculated to inspire terror in anyone who knew himself to be their enemy whether declared or secret.

While this state of fear and confusion reigned in the city, Monseigneur de Bourbon, whose troops were scattered among various fortresses in the Valdarno, learned in a letter from the viceroy that the pope had refused to sign the final version of the accord and that all the forces of the League were encamped near Florence. Bourbon could see no way that his army, worn out hungry and lacking both supplies and munitions, could approach our walls. So he left Montevarchi and repositioned his army in Sienese territory. He declared that he wanted to rest and feed his army there so that he could plunder our domains with greater facility and in better order. He also said that if he were backed with Sienese artillery and munitions he would attempt to take Florence. Nonetheless, recognizing the difficulties and dangers these plans entailed, he assembled all the Spanish and German officers in his quarters and in a long speech (having first described to them the condition and situation of the army) tried to convince them that of the three courses that were open to them, he could see no better option than to march immediately on Rome. To stay too long in Sienese territory would be the worst course, he argued, since the damage caused by such a large army and the impossibility of supplying it for any length of time would soon alienate a friendly population. And in addition this delay would give the enemy ample time to organize and prepare for its defense. Marching on Florence, on the other hand, either to besiege the city or to pillage the countryside, would be a difficult and dangerous undertaking. Although the city was well provisioned, it was heavily defended. The Florentine countryside had been sacked already, and the people had taken refuge in fortified places. Tuscany is mountainous in any case and difficult to maneuver in.

Marching with all possible speed on Rome however, he argued, would be a course that was safe, glorious, and rewarding. Knowing the pope to be lacking in everything necessary to his defense, Cardinal Colonna had written to Bourbon, urging him to march without losing further time and assuring him that his faction in Rome was entirely favorable to Caesar. Bourbon also pointed out that it would be impossible for the League army to reach Rome as quickly as the imperial forces could. The League forces were camped further away, dispersed in various locations, and commanded by different officers. If they started out in pursuit, they would be forced to take a longer road. Consequently, taking the rich city of Rome would be much easier if they exerted themselves and reached it with a speed that was beyond the expectations of the pope and the cardinals.

"If His Holiness thinks," Bourbon argued, "that our glorious army cannot attack him because of the nearness of the forces of the League, he will make no preparations whatsoever for his defense. In fact, he will probably be convinced that the difficulties of our situation will force us to ask for peace on the terms that he has conceived and communicated to us repeatedly through the viceroy. And even though our difficulties seem very great, it cannot be denied that the greater they seem, the more we must force ourselves to choose a course that will diminish them or cancel them entirely, as will be the case if we march immediately on Rome. The Sienese will give us provisions more willingly since we will be distancing ourselves from them; and in a short time we will find ourselves attacking that most illustrious city, with no impediment from outside and little resistance from those within – a most rare opportunity and one to spur on even a weak army, let alone a ferocious one like this. For many reasons, then, I foresee an easy and very rewarding victory. In order to achieve it, though, the army must forget about past difficulties and those that we must endure in the little bit of the journey that remains and march with all speed to the walls of Rome."

These and many other arguments, very effectively presented by Bourbon, persuaded these lords and officers to favor the attack on Rome over all other plans. Because they were convinced, it was much easier for them to persuade the rest of the army afterwards. When he realized that everyone was in favor of his idea, Bourbon had all the prisoners who had been captured in various places along their line of march brought before him. Up till that time they had been kept in chains. After they had been liberated and unchained, (even though there was a large number of them) he addressed them in a very friendly way:

"If you wish either to return to your homes or come with this glorious army to Rome, you are free to do so. No one will stop you from leaving or prevent you from joining the company of these foreigners. On my honor, I promise you that if you follow us faithfully, you will be our companions in every victory and share in the sack of Rome."

After these words the majority of the younger prisoners eagerly joined the army, and the others returned without hindrance to their homes. And then, on the very same day, which was the twenty-seventh of April, having agreed with the government of Siena on the amount of daily provisions they would need, they started out immediately for Rome by the shortest route and without any artillery to slow them down. They soon reached the river Paglia, which was very swollen from the recent rains. After several soldiers had waded across with difficulty and the loss of some men, they crossed it in this fashion: the infantry broke down into groups of thirty to fifty men who held each other by the arms and hands and crossed the river linked together in this way. Some were in water up to their chests, many up to their necks, and when the current pushed with extra force against one of them he would be swept away; but then the others would regroup quickly in the same fashion. Aided by the strongest and most courageous, they reached the other side with few losses. The cavalry had already arrived there with light casualties, even though many infantry crossed with them by hanging onto the neck, mane, or tail of a horse. After relaxing a little and regrouping, they continued their march with the same speed and good order. Along the way they sacked only Montefiasconi and Ronciglione when they refused provisions and passage to the army. To avoid losing time, they did no damage to the other towns and fortresses they came upon.

When their unexpected departure and the source of their supplies were learned of in Florence, the lieutenant-general immediately ordered a large part of the Black Bands, which was then in San Casciano, to march towards Arezzo. He alerted Count Guido Rangoni and advised him to take those troops and his cavalry at a forced march by the Perugia road to Rome. He emphasized how necessary it was that he arrive in Rome before the enemy. He knew that the pope was not expecting Bourbon to attack and that he was entirely lacking the forces he needed in this very dangerous turn of events. Then the lieutenant-general, along with the other agents of the pope, dispatched several messengers to His Holiness informing him of the movement of the imperial army, its speed, and the source of its supplies. They also informed him that forces under Count Guido Rangoni had been dispatched and that they were expected to arrive in Rome before the enemy. With great urgency they requested the duke of Urbino, the marquis of Saluzzo, and the Venetian quartermaster-general, who were then in Florence, to dispatch the rest of the forces of the League immediately, so that the enemy could not remain unchallenged for a single day at the walls of Rome.

But all this care on the part of the officers of the Church was in vain. This time the duke of Urbino betrayed his true motives to those who were still doubtful. He took more time leaving Florence than the urgency of the situation permitted; and he allowed his men to do worse damage wherever they passed through our territory than the Germans. He delayed the march as much as he could on one pretext or another, so that it was no surprise that he was still ten miles from Lake Trasimene when Bourbon arrived at the walls of Rome on the fifth of May, 1527, at 5:00 PM, with his entire army, but with such a severe shortage of supplies that he couldn't have lasted there for two days.

As soon as he arrived he ordered (as is the military custom) that the pope be requested to allow the imperial army passage through the city. He declared that he only wanted to lead his forces to Naples. His demand (following the customary form) was denied. This left him no way to go forward, since many of his troops, who had already attempted to cross the Tiber in boats had been lost, and others skirmishing at the walls had had no success.

Realizing the difficulties and dangers his army faced, he immediately called together the officers of the infantry and cavalry. After describing the army's extreme lack of food, munitions, and money, he tried his best to persuade them not to wait until morning, but to attack immediately with every ounce of their energy, and force their way over the walls. Their arrival had not been expected either by the pope or the people, and so it was reasonable to assume that those within were not prepared for them either physically or in spirit, and not in any way organized for battle. But, if they waited until tomorrow to fight, those within, anticipating the attack, would have time during the night to organize and prepare themselves. Therefore, if they attacked now, victory would be sure and easy, but tomorrow it would be difficult and very dangerous. This was an opportunity that no prudent man would let slip by. Such a man only differs from ordinary men in knowing how to seize opportunity by the forelock when it suddenly appears. He went on to say that while he realized that the army was exhausted and badly in need of rest, nonetheless, because the victory would be easy, everyone should spur himself on to make a final try. Encouraged by their officers, the troops could be persuaded to lose no time in bringing this glorious undertaking to its conclusion. With these and similar arguments he urged the leaders and commanders to arouse the courage and determination of their troops. But he soon realized that his arguments had not persuaded the officers of the army to attack immediately. Given their reluctance, he saw no alternative but to attack the following morning at first light, and then to make every effort they could without artillery to break into Rome.

Disguising his disappointment, he had most of the army assembled before sunset; and after climbing up to some high place, he made the following speech:

"My dearest lords and fellow soldiers, if I didn't have proof through long experience of your courage and strength, and if I didn't know how easily Rome can be taken, I would address you differently right now. I would use the words that many emperors in many less serious situations have spoken to their troops. Once encouraged and excited by them, these men have gone on to easy victory. But because I am certain that such words would only be adding flame to fire, I will let them go. I know that men in superior armies have no need of urging, and I know, too, that hardships and dangers much worse than the present ones would not intimidate you.

"Indeed I cannot imagine what sufferings could be worse than those which you have borne so courageously already, considering the intolerable fatigue, poverty, and hunger that with unfailing and manly stamina, fellow soldiers, you have endured for many months in order to reach these walls. How lightly you bear the incredible strains you are undergoing right now, here in a place where there is no more food nor hope of having it immediately (as we must) from any direction. To turn back, we cannot and must not consider; to cross the Tiber, except through Rome, is impossible. We have little ammunition and no artillery. If we are not surrounded by the enemy, that is not only because they lack manliness and courage, but also because their leaders believe that our situation is so hopeless that they will be victorious without bloodying their swords.

"Now, even though our danger is great – and it is clear that no superlative army of the past ever faced such a crisis – nonetheless you must also realize that no nation was ever offered an easier, more deserved, or richer prize. I say 'easy' because where I will lead you to make your assault,

artillery won't be necessary. Simply by your skill and determination, you will overcome their ramparts and bastions.
Easy, too, since there are no more than three thousand
troops inside these walls, mere recruits at that, and
unaccustomed to wounds and death. In addition to these
advantages, Cardinal Colonna has written me again just
a few hours ago, in these letters which I am holding up to
show you, to say that the Ghibelline party could not be
more willing to give us its complete support, since they
are very eager for our victory.

"Why I say 'rich' you can easily understand, for enclosed within these walls, which you must now assault,
there are, in addition to the pope, many cardinals, prelates, lords, courtiers, merchants, as well as the barons and
people of Rome, all possessing untold riches. None of
them imagined that this luckiest of armies would have
enough courage to attack Rome, and that the army of
the League would not be here to keep us company (as
they have been everywhere else). Words cannot express the
sorrow and dismay that are in their hearts right now. Not
only because they are cowardly by nature and habit, but
because they expect, and with good reason, from the great
and most just God (since they have been abandoned by
their own army) the punishment and scourge that their
evil customs and irreligious lives have deserved for so
long. With the greatest justice this punishment has been
postponed until this blessed day and left to the Spanish
and German nations by Him who gives all things being
and maintains them in motion.

"And even though Rome's inestimable wealth of gold
and silver will in part reward your courageous efforts, it
cannot measure up to your invincible daring and courage.
For when I look into your faces, lords and fellows soldiers,
I plainly see that it would be much more to your liking if
waiting for you in Rome were one of those emperors to
whom the name Germanicus was given in arrogance,
along with his chosen legions. Men who spilled the blood

of your innocent ancestors both in your country and in Italy through a thousand subterfuges and betrayals. Such a desire is very honorable and entirely in keeping with your greatness and nobility. But since Nature has changed human culture over the long course of time, there is such a dissolute way of life at present in that city that it is no wonder that there are no just or virtuous men in Rome. None ready to show their faces and their swords to the enemy; and none who are accustomed to rule virtuously (as they used to do) over distant countries. Nowadays they are immersed in lustful and effeminate pastimes, and totally committed to amassing silver and gold with fraud, pillage, and cruelty, under the banner of Christian piety.

"Since therefore, lords and fellow soldiers, you cannot avenge the injuries of the past, or in any way measure the aggressiveness and military perfection of this invincible army against the ancient Romans, you must take whatever revenge you can. And when our emperor learns that the pope and all of Rome are in your hands, he can swiftly come here, not only to reward your virtues abundantly, but to lead you (after he has taken Italy and France) against the Infidel, and to range with you in victory through Asia and Africa. There and then you will have a thousand opportunities to show the whole universe that you have far surpassed the glory and riches of the incomparable armies of Darius, Alexander the Great, or any other ruler known to history.

"Among the Spaniards in this army are some who have seen a New World, which is already entirely obedient to our invincible Majesty, Caesar. Once Rome is taken, as I hope she will be, only a little remains to complete his conquest of the Western Hemisphere. And when I begin to imagine this in the future, I seem to see all of you shining in golden armor, all lords and princes of conquered lands that you have received in gift from our most liberal emperor. For of this universal triumph and of the imminent conquest of Rome, our infallible prophet, Martin Luther, has spoken many times.

"Remember, my lords, that some of you were present when the king of France was taken and his army destroyed. Remember when you held the people of Milan by force, despite the presence of the whole army of the League. Those who have only recently come into Italy have conquered and killed Signor Giovanni de' Medici and with great endurance overcome the difficulties of the terrain and the continual rain and snow. Let these new men know that the compensation for the scarcity and poverty you have endured (for those who do not wish to march further with the army) is to have the abundance and wealth of Rome to use any way you like. You must realize though, that the famous victories and outstanding achievements of this extraordinary army will all turn sour and come to nothing if, when you are given the signal to attack Rome, you do not force yourselves to do all that the present grave situation requires, and all that the certainty of future wealth inspires."

Before Bourbon had reached the end of his speech, a certain light and vigorous murmuring began to be heard among the army. It could easily be seen by this that every hour before the assault began would seem a hundred to that multitude. When Bourbon saw everyone so willing and eager, he praised them again in a few words, and gently reminded them that they should get whatever sleep and refreshment they could during the night so that they would be well prepared at first light for the assault on the walls. Then he assigned them to their camps and went off to confer again with the colonels and other leaders of the army. After talking and arguing for most of the night, they decided where and how they should attack at dawn. Before he dismissed them, Bourbon reminded them that above everything else the officers were to instill in their troops the idea that victory was certain.

While the imperials outside were wasting no time, in Rome, when such a large number of the enemy had appeared at the walls, despite the general opinion that this was impossible, there were many who thought that this must be the army of the League. In fact they hadn't even heard of the departure of the imperial forces from Siena before the enemy had reached Viterbo. Others thought about how to protect themselves from imminent peril. The pope, who was entirely without supplies and disarmed, had no time to search for troops in the areas where good and courageous ones are to be found. Consequently he was forced in furious haste to arm about three thousand artisans, servants, and other simple people unaccustomed to hearing drums with arms in their hands, let alone artillery. In this emergency His Holiness suddenly realized what a grave error it had been to release his Swiss soldiers and those two thousand men of the Black Bands, in order (as Jacopo Salviati used to say) to save 30,000 scudi a month.

In the crisis he gave orders that those ramparts that had been built at other times were to be restored as quickly as possible, that artillery was to be brought to specified places, munitions distributed in an orderly fashion, and that available soldiers were to be assigned to the walls and to the weakest points. He also ordered a large band of men to be stationed in an appropriate place so that they could come to the aid of any part of the city that was in need. He appointed someone to administer the food supplies and other things necessary for the combatants; he also ordered fires to be lit and flammable mixtures prepared that were to be thrown on the enemy when they approached the walls or wherever else they were needed.

Despite the confusion, the Holy Father was called on to comfort many people, which he did by explaining the difficulties the enemy faced with regard to money and supplies, and how they could not capture a little fortress without artillery, as they had shown again and again on the march, let alone Rome. He said that when they were repulsed on their first assault, they would be forced by hunger and by fear of the League army, which was already nearby, to break up on their own. He comforted them, too, with the idea that since the enemy were Lutherans, God could only have led them for a mysterious purpose to the very capital of His holy religion, in order to have them all cut to pieces in a notorious and exemplary way. Finally he promised (as is the ridiculous custom of pontiffs in such situations) with great solemnity to those who fought valorously and were killed, in addition to passing on their benefices and ecclesiastical offices to their next of kin, a plenary remission of all their sins.

Recognizing the poor quality of his officers and the indifference of troops recruited so haphazardly, His Holiness was more inclined to abandon Rome (seeing it in such confusion) than to defend it; nonetheless, persuaded and restrained by his expert advisors, he remained and encouraged others to stay. And if His Holiness had been permitted by his sacred office personally to inspect the walls and ramparts, the artillery, and other things necessary for the defense of Rome, without doubt they would have been organized differently than they were by the likes of Signor Renzo and the others who had charge of them. But out of respect for his position as Vicar of Christ on Earth, he was forced to trust to the eyes and minds of his officers. The example of His Blessedness should teach every prince how little he should delegate to his subordinates in critical situations.

The Roman people and resident aliens, who had taken a census of themselves a few days before that totaled about thirty-thousand combatants, considered themselves invincible, the way people usually do before they look danger in the face. More often than any other officer of Our Lord, Signor Renzo da Ceri declared his opinion that the enemy could not last two days outside the walls because of their extreme lack of food; and that on the second day the army of the League would enter Rome. This made the people feel even more secure. The datary, too, and Jacopo Salviati, along with many others, were so certain of victory that not only would they not permit the pope to leave, but they also prevented the merchants from Florence and other places from putting their wives and their most valuable goods into a galleon and various other ships, which they had hired for the purpose, and sending them immediately towards Civitavecchia. Instead they had the gates of the city closed. They declared that such fears were ridiculous and unnecessary, and that this was no time to permit things that could cause panic among those who remained in the city. They also argued that it would increase the hopes and stubbornness of the enemy, if they saw people fleeing and goods being shipped out. As a result of these arguments, it seems that the majority in Rome anticipated the assault on the walls without fear.

I do not want to omit the story of a man who had appeared in Rome several days before this. He was from the Sienese countryside, of middle age and very humble background, with red skin, naked and emaciated, and, from what it appeared, very religious. He had publicly predicted to the whole Roman population that the destruction of the priests and of the entire city was certain and that a renewal of the Church was at hand. He had often described in terrifying terms the coming of the time of penitence for, as he said, he saw the scourge very near. In the presence of many people he had spoken contemptuously to the pope and, in very insulting and crude terms, had predicted that God would destroy him. Because of this he was in prison at that time, where, with greater insistence than before, he repeated the same statements. A very small number of people (as always happens in such cases) believed him.

I could also describe some portents that were noted not long before this in Rome, which signified massive and speedy destruction: such as the birth of a mule in the Cancelleria, and the spontaneous collapse of a section of wall that united the papal palace with Castel Sant' Angelo. I am restrained, however, by my knowledge that not everyone judges such extraordinary events to have any meaning, even though ancient and modern histories are full of very similar incidents that preceded disasters or the destruction of cities. One also reads that fear of these portents led many Christian peoples as well as Gentiles to placate the just wrath of Highest Jove with sacrifices and devout ceremonies whenever they appeared. God's mercy seems to reach out to mortals with divers and terrible signs before their punishment and to try to bring them back to a better life through the fear inspired by such signs, rather than with justice.

Despite the skepticism of some, I cannot refrain from describing two very obvious portents that occurred not many months before in Rome. The first was a lightning bolt that lifted the Infant from the arms of a highly revered statue of Our Lady in the church of S. Maria in Trastevere. The Child was broken to pieces, and Our Lady's crown was stricken, shattered, and thrown to the ground. The second portent involved a Eucharistic wafer that had been deposited in a tabernacle of the chapel of the pope on Holy Thursday, as is customary at that period. It was found the following morning thrown to the ground, without evidence of why or by whom this was done.

These are strong signs that might reasonably frighten any Christian, for the celestial fire had stricken and destroyed the image of the human origin of Our Savior and shamefully broken the glorious crown of His Most Holy Mother. About two months before that the consecrated Host, which we Christians so rightfully adore, refused to remain where it had rested for many and many a year before at the same period. But because they were entirely blinded and immersed in lust, avarice, and ambition, the hearts of the Scribes and the Pharisees of that city were too hardened for these divine manifestations to affect.

While preparations were being made inside and outside Rome, the dawn of May 6 was approaching. Almost everything was already in order in the imperial army, and a large detachment of troops was approaching that part of the city wall near Santo Spirito. Monseigneur de Bourbon, all in armor with a loose white coat worn over it, was continually to be seen riding here and there on horseback, comforting and encouraging his troops. To the Spanish and German veterans of Milan, he would say: "Now for the third time you must show that strength and ferocity that we have seen in you twice before; for the riches and the glory that you earned in those victories will be lost – as well as your lives – if your energy flags at this point." He told the Italians that it was every bit as necessary to show their valor at this point as it had been in their other campaigns. If they didn't win today, they would be better off taking their own lives than falling into the hands of the enemy. There was nowhere for them to go, he said, for those in this incomparable army stood alone against all the forces of the League. Beyond this, he offered again what he had promised them so many times before, declaring that in addition to their portion of the booty, they would become lords and rulers of their native cities and towns.

To the Lutherans who had come with Captain von Frundsberg, he recalled the great discomforts, the intolerable hunger, and the extreme lack of money that they had endured for no other purpose than to reach the walls of Rome. And if they showed the fire he knew they had in them, it was certain that in a very few hours they would be inside the city with their wives and children. Then they would be rich and secure, enjoying the incredible wealth of vicious and ridiculous prelates. And continually riding through the camp, wherever he saw a large number of armed men together, he approached to give them comfort and encourage them to go forward. Again and again he promised that he was going to be among the first to climb over those famous walls. By his readiness and courage, he tried to show the army that he thought victory was certain. As a result of his care and encouragement, the infantry and cavalry forces were in order before dawn, no less eager than ready to attack energetically.

The Spanish (as is their custom) had already begun to attack the city with great boldness from several directions. Making the least possible noise, however, a large number of them were concentrating on trying to enter the city at a point near Santo Spirito above the gardens of Cardinal Armellini, since the walls were lower there than elsewhere. In that place the circuit of the walls incorporated the main wall of a small private house. This had been done in such a way that the thinness and weakness of the wall would be invisible either from within or from without to anyone who didn't look very carefully. In that wall there was a cannon port that was wider than the usual dimensions, which had been adapted from a window of that house. In addition to this, also in the thin part of the wall, right against the ground, but covered outside with dirt and manure, there was a little window, which had opened into the basement of that structure. It was not barred but only closed up with wood so that the necessary light could enter. At that time it no longer served to let light into the cellar, and it was covered and hidden so that it would not be visible unless someone paid particular attention to it. Nonetheless it cannot be denied that its existence represented a very serious oversight, and one that cannot be excused for any reason on the part of Signor Renzo or Giuliano Leno, or whoever was assigned to survey the walls and other points of attack. It would have been easy for anyone who had imagination to discover it, even if he lacked military experience. It should have been especially obvious to those who consider themselves more expert than others in the fortification of cities. Coming upon this little house built into the city walls, the Roman officers should have examined it inside and out with particular care in order to discover these weak points. They should not have passed over it inattentively as they did.

By this example one can see that officials and officers are like the people who appoint them, and that the wisdom of the superior is revealed by those who carry out his orders. For the mind of the employee corresponds to that of his superior. In important situations one should rely very little on the eyes and intellect of his subordinates. The errors they make cannot be corrected when the situation becomes critical; and the shame and the damage rest completely on the shoulders of the superior who allows himself to be governed by his men. In this instance, though, one cannot entirely blame Pope Clement. Even though His Holiness knew the virtues and defects of his officers perfectly well and had very little confidence in their diligence, nonetheless His Beatitude was handicapped by not being able (given his supreme position) personally to examine the walls, ramparts, and other things necessary for defense; and so he had to rely on incompetents.

Towards this part of the wall then (perhaps its weakness and that opening had already been noticed), the Spanish made a concentrated advance in an effort to force an entry. Just about this time a heavy fog began to appear, which spread itself thickly over the ground and became increasingly dense as day approached. This often happens in the middle of Spring; and this fog was so thick that people could not see each other at a distance of six feet. Because it was necessary to go more by hearing than by sight in the dense fog and to fire towards the noise made by the enemy, the artillery of Castel Sant' Angelo and other batteries in Rome could do no damage to the enemy except by chance. For this reason the majority of shots fired from within did as much harm to the defenders as they did to the enemy, or they hit nothing at all.

Meanwhile the imperial army fiercely attacked and forced itself relentlessly (ignoring the obvious dangers) to scale the walls. Monseigneur de Bourbon was to be seen encouraging the troops and (as many have described) holding onto one of the ladders leaning against the wall with his left hand, and with his right hand signaling and urging the men to ascend it. Suddenly he was shot through by a ball from an arquebus, and he fell mortally wounded. There are those who report that while he was dying he said, "Cover me up, soldiers, so that the enemy doesn't learn of my death, and continue the battle courageously. My death cannot deprive you of so sure and hard-won a victory." Others, though, describe his death in other terms.

He was an outstanding officer and because of his liberality, his intelligence, and his courage he is to be numbered among the truly great. When news of such an unexpected tragedy spread among the leaders of the army, it caused such anguish that the violence and force of the attack abated somewhat. They knew they had suffered a terrible loss, and one that could seriously weaken their chances of victory. Nonetheless, realizing that the conquered have no salvation but to expect none, after hastily taking counsel among themselves, they concluded that they had no better hope than to try their luck once more with even greater boldness. Since they were desperate, their natural ferocity came out more strongly and with greater violence. They attacked the same section of the wall once again in greater force, making a fierce effort to breach it; and the heavy fog continued in their favor. Despite the defense from within, they never retreated an inch or slowed down their furious attack. In grave danger now, the defenders repeatedly threw burning liquids over the wall and fired continually with artillery, arquebuses, and other firearms towards the noise made by the enemy. They fought like this on both sides for another hour without stopping. This was less difficult for the imperial troops, however, who were in large enough numbers so that they could spell each other. When one company of them had fired their arquebuses, or were fatigued enough to need a rest, another fresh squad took their places and continued the attack. Seeing the force and strength of the enemy continually increasing and neither hearing or seeing their furor abating anywhere (even though they had pushed them from the walls various times and even captured some of their ensigns), those within began to be fearful and doubtful of victory.

At ten o'clock a small band of Spanish troops was seen inside the city; but the rest of the army was unaware of this. They had either widened the cannon-port with sticks and iron picks, or entered by the cellar window mentioned above. Many were convinced, however, that the first troops entered Rome somewhere between Porta Torrione and Santo Spirito, where the walls are lower than elsewhere. By what means such a small number of Spaniards could have entered so easily, I will leave for others to sort out among so many different opinions. I will only say that since no other part of the wall was knocked down except that little bit where the cannon-port and the cellar window had been broken out and enlarged, many people are inclined to believe that the Spanish first gained entry through that window, especially since their first incursion was achieved with such speed and ease.

The first to realize that the Spaniards were inside (as many confirm) was Signor Renzo, who immediately called out in a loud voice, "The enemy are within! Save yourselves, retreat to the strongest and safest places!" Words (if they were indeed spoken by him) hardly befitting an officer, who instead should have immediately organized his troops into the strongest force possible and charged with them against the enemy. Then with all the courage and violence that were required in this climactic moment, his men should have pushed and shoved them with force outside the walls. This is what many men in such crises have been able to do.

But no sooner had he pronounced those weak and terrifying words (as those who were then in his presence have told me), than he retreated at a run towards the Ponte Sant' Angelo. He was immediately followed by everyone who was around him in a state of confusion and terror of the kind that always accompanies impulsiveness and disorder. He reached the bridge at the same time as many other soldiers and Roman civilians who had abandoned the ramparts when they heard he had fled. They had been listening as the enemy yelled continually, "Spain! Spain! Kill! Kill!" When they had all crossed the Tiber with great difficulty, they mixed in with the confused and disorderly crowd on the other side. Those who could not get across the Tiber, either because terror had incapacitated them or because of the great mob that got in everyone's way as it ran here and there, retreated to Castel Sant' Angelo. A little while before Our Lord had entered the castello in furious haste. He found no supplies, nor any of the other things necessary to sustain life or to repel the enemy (though he had long before ordered that they be stocked). Immediately he had whatever supplies and munitions were to be had in that state of confusion brought in from the houses and shops that were nearby.

But while these arrangements were being made inside the castello, a crowd of prelates, merchants, nobles, courtiers, women, and soldiers gathered at the principal entrance, mixed up and pressed together so tightly that they prevented the closing of the gate. Finally those inside dropped the portcullis, even though it slid down and was secured only with great difficulty because it had not been inspected earlier and cleaned of rust. Those without were forced to accept the fact that if they wished to save themselves, they would have to go elsewhere. There were already more than three thousand people inside the castello. A large number of important people, prelates, and other notables were among them, plus all the cardinals except for Valle, Aracoeli, Cesarini, Siena, and Enckenvoirt. Because they were leaders of the Ghibelline faction, these cardinals thought they would be more secure in their own palaces and didn't want to be enclosed in the castello.

As he approached the castello at a run, Cardinal Pucci was trampled and badly wounded in the head and shoulders by the terrified crowd on the bridge. After great labors by his servants, he was let in, more than half dead, through a window that was unbarred. Cardinal Armellini, who was unable to enter the castello with the others, had himself hauled up in a basket on cables dropped from above. There he found Jacopo Salviati, the archbishop of Capua, the datary, Signor Alberto da Carpi, Signor Orazio Baglioni, and many other nobles, in such terror and distress as can easily be imagined, for they had expected anything but this disaster.

Meanwhile the rest of the Roman people, as well as the merchants, prelates, courtiers, and foreigners all ran back and forth in great confusion and terror looking for some refuge. Running through the streets as if they were lost, unable to leave Rome because the gates were barred, they entered the strongest places or those they considered the safest. Some took refuge in the Colonna houses, others in those of the Spanish, Flemish, and Germans who had lived for many years in Rome, and many others in the palaces of Cardinals Enckenvoirt, Aracoeli, Siena, Cesarini, and Valle.

Since it is an especially noteworthy fact, I must include here that in this calamity for themselves and for their unlucky city none of those appointed to be officers of the Church made any attempt to cut the bridges or to organize the defense of the walls of Trastevere. They did not, as they should have, resist with all their strength the attack of their cruel enemy or resolve to die manfully defending themselves with weapons in their hands, rather than to fall in a shameful, cowardly way into the hands of the brutal victors. Instead, running like everyone else, they increased the panic in Rome and gave the enemy confidence of absolute victory.

Among these captains, the one everyone blames most is Signor Renzo. He had been more confident of victory than anyone else; he was the leader of the Guelfs, and he was supported by many Romans in arms. But he did not take those measures which could have been effective if done quickly and could have saved the major part of Rome. Instead, without consulting the officers or the people who were there, he ran into the castello in great fear and agitation like the others. But he is not the only one guilty of such gross incompetence. All who were in command should have come together and with courage and self-sacrifice found a way to defend the city and everyone's property.

It would have been easy to defend Rome itself if, using all the speed and courage required, they had filled the Ponte Sisto with wood, set it afire, and cut it. (This is what the Romans did after they had retreated to the far side when they saw Horatius Coccles single-handedly keeping the enemy from crossing.) Had the bridge been cut, within a few days the imperial army would have been in the same difficulties inside Trastevere as they had been in before they invaded Rome. In fact, being continually battered by the artillery of the castello, they would have been in greater danger there.

A few hours after the entry of the enemy into the city, Count Guido Rangoni with his cavalry and soldiers of the Black Bands arrived at Monte Rotondo. They could have entered the city easily through the Porta del Popolo, and would undoubtedly have hurt and hampered the enemy. They would also have given encouragement to the forces of the League who were still en route and increased their willingness to show themselves at the walls of Rome. Through their intervention, too, the pontiff could have been liberated more easily and with greater safety. Whether His Holiness had more reason to grieve for his officers than for his own situation, I will let others decide: their failings were outrageous, but he had yielded to persuasion and stayed in the city against his better judgment.

But returning to the invasion of the imperial army: when the Spaniards saw Signor Renzo fleeing so timidly, along with all those who were assigned to defend the walls and the ramparts, they immediately called in the bulk of the Spanish forces who were still outside the city. Together they formed a unified and well-organized attack force that was determined to make full use of its advantage. Their only goal was to kill whomever they encountered. Any soldier or officer of the Church whom they overtook (because he was not among the cowards who fled immediately), recognizing no other way to save his own life, in the confusion blended in with the victors and joined them in pursuing those who fled. Thus in a very short time, the imperial forces took the Borgo and Trastevere, suffering very few casualties in the process. Having killed about a thousand of the defenders, they were able to establish control over the others who lived there. Meanwhile in a great rush the rest of the army swarmed in, climbing over the low places in the walls and the abandoned ramparts. They also entered through Porta S. Pancrazio, which had been beaten in and shattered. Once inside, they paused awhile to recover their strength and to refresh themselves with the abundance of food that they found there.

In this early stage of their invasion, they seemed willing to come to an agreement with the pope; they said it was because of the loss of Bourbon and their other diffi-

culties. His Holiness treated this offer with the credulous-
ness that is common in disasters and in those situations
were great hopes are aroused. He had immediately dispatched the ambassador of Portugal, with whom the
Spanish officers were negotiating the terms of an agreement. These officers seemed to be negotiating in good
faith, despite what many in the castello thought at first,
even though the imperial forces were already in control
of part of the city and facing no opposition. Because they
were unable to assess the situation in the city as a whole,
and whether or not they were going to be able to cross the
Tiber, the officers were pretending to be inclined towards
an agreement. But after some insincere negotiation with
the pope's representative, the Spanish and Germans, who
had conferred by then, decided that they wouldn't waste
any more time or worry about being tired and hungry.
Once they had discovered how confused and vulnerable
the city was, they decided that they would take the rest of
it immediately.

And so with a great noise of drums and trumpets, and
with other military sounds calculated to terrify anyone
not used to hearing them, they marched boldly at 6:00 PM
towards the gate house of the Ponte Sisto. They had earlier dispatched about a thousand arquebusiers in complete
silence to surprise the forces they assumed would be there
to defend it. Instead they found it nearly abandoned and
with very few defenders, since everyone was confused and
fearful; and so they captured it without difficulty. Afterwards, without losing time, as soon as the main body of
the army had arrived, they marched towards the Ponte
Sisto. They crossed it in good order and with a great show
of ferocity, although they met little resistance. Then they
immediately spread out through the streets on the other
side. Killing anyone they encountered, they began a terrifying slaughter. But since there was no one who resisted
their fury, in a short while they became masters of this

ancient, noble city, full of all the riches that the greediest and hungriest army could desire.

When they realized that all the defenders had fled and that they were truly in control of the city, the Spanish troops began to capture houses (along with everyone and everything that was in them) and to take prisoners. Those that they came upon as they fled in confusion through the streets, they also took captive rather than killing them. The Germans, however, were obeying the articles of war and cutting to pieces anyone they came upon (an act that is very necessary in the first hours of a victory). When they saw how the Spanish were acting, the Germans began to fear betrayal. They were quickly persuaded, however, by the Spanish captains that since the city was abandoned by its defenders, and that great riches must have been hidden in it, it would be a grave mistake not to keep alive anyone who might be able to show them where treasures were hidden or give them the names of people outside Rome who would pay their ransoms.

So then the lancers also began to take captive whomever they encountered and to break into the most beautiful houses they saw. And in a short time nearly everyone was taken prisoner, for they had no respect for the sacred places where (as always in such crises) many women, children, and frightened men had taken refuge. Divine things were treated no differently by them than profane ones. And rushing continually here and there like Furies from hell, they searched every sacred place and, with terrible violence, broke into any building they chose. Wherever they encountered resistance, they fought with ferocity; and if they could not overcome the defenders, they set the place on fire. Many priceless objects and many people who would not surrender themselves into their bestial hands were burned and consumed.

How many courtiers, how many genteel and cultivated men, how many refined prelates, how many devoted nuns, virgins, or chaste wives with their little children became the prey of these cruel foreigners! How many calixes, crosses, statues, and vessels of silver and gold were stolen from the altars, sacristies, and other holy places where they were stored. How many rare and venerable relics, covered with gold and silver, were despoiled by bloody, homicidal hands and hurled with impious derision to the earth. The heads of St. Peter, St. Paul, St. Andrew and many other saints; the wood of the Cross, the Thorns, the Holy Oil, and even consecrated Hosts were shamefully trodden underfoot in that fury.

In the street you saw nothing but thugs and rogues carrying great bundles of the richest vestments and ecclesiastical ornaments and huge sacks full of all kinds of vessels of gold and silver – testifying more to the riches and empty pomp of the Roman curia than to the humble poverty and true devotion of the Christian religion. Great numbers of captives of all sorts were to be seen, groaning and screaming, being swiftly led to makeshift prisons. In the streets there were many corpses. Many nobles lay there cut to pieces, covered with mud and their own blood, and many people only half dead lay miserably on the ground. Sometimes in that ghastly scene a child or man would be seen jumping from a window, forced to jump or jumping voluntarily to escape becoming the living prey of these monsters and finally ending their lives horribly in the street.

It did the Colonna and the Ghibellines no good to be of that faction, because the victors had no more regard for that party than for the other; nor did they treat the Spaniards, the Germans, and the Flemish who had lived a long time in Rome any better than any Italian courtier or clergyman. Those cardinals who had not taken refuge in the castello received no respect or deference; even though they had convinced themselves beforehand that they would be well treated because of their dignity, their extraordinary costumes, and the fact that they were no less wicked than the other leaders of the imperial party.

Instead they were quickly made prisoners in their own palaces along with all those who had taken refuge there for their own safety.

The naiveté and miscalculation of these people clearly demonstrate how much effect the love of a faction can have on the minds of its partisans. Trusting to factional loyalty against all reason and experience, they put themselves into the power of men who were sworn enemies of Italy and extremely envious of their wealth. Imagine what fury, what turmoil, and what violence there were in that miserable city, the victim of two such starved and bestial enemies, who competed with each other in robbery and the display of cruelty. It is likely that this time even Spanish greed and German rage were completely sated.

If I were to describe in detail the various and strange events that happened while the victors swept on in their raging fury, it would be to write not one but many terrifying tragedies. By those accounts, it is true, one would better understand the greed and cruelty of soldiers who take a city by force, having defeated it at the risk of their own blood. Nonetheless, to avoid repetition, I shall only describe one such event, no less absurd than terrible, and by its characteristics you can easily imagine the horrible qualities of the other events that took place in that time of fury.

While this army of foreigners were scurrying here and there, looting and killing, and entering every storehouse and shop, about ten Spaniards happened to find themselves together inside a shop full of merchandise, and they began to rummage through it. One of them came upon a huge number of worthless metal slugs or counters in a sack, and blinded by greed and fury, imagined that they were gold ducats. He let the rest of them know what he had found, and they quickly locked themselves inside the shop. Since they didn't want to share the treasure, which they imagined they had found, with others, they made a determined effort to keep everyone else out of the shop.

A company of Germans happened along and seeing such care being taken by those within to prevent anyone from entering, they concluded that the cause was the abundance of the booty (which it was). Rather than waste time, they set the shop on fire, declaring that it was unfair that the lancers should win the war, while the Spanish alone enjoyed the spoils. And before they left they had burned the shop with just about everyone and everything in it – a fitting punishment for the insatiable greed of the Spanish, but one that exemplifies the raging fury of the Germans as well.

Carrying on in this fashion, the foreign conquerors attended to nothing but catering to and satiating their outrageous appetites, often to their own harm. (All this happened before the eyes of the Holy Father, of Jacopo Salviati, of Cardinal Armellini, Signor Renzo, the datary, and Signor Alberto. In different ways each of these men was responsible for the shameful and disastrous sack that was occurring.)

Through no lack of energy on their part, or prisoners or booty, the imperial forces brought the looting to a halt after three days. This happened because the conquerors (having failed to rob and pillage various foreign prelates) began to turn against each other with equal rapacity and violence. The more prudent officers quickly realized how crucial it was to put an end to this insatiable predation. They realized how much disorder this unrestrained violence towards their own could cause, especially since they held a very large number of prisoners, and the army of the League was approaching Rome. So they deputized various men who commanded respect among this band of thieves and authorized them to punish atrociously those who would not obey. In this way they put a stop to the killing that had sprung up among them. They also agreed to retire to the areas they had captured to rest and enjoy their prizes. Meanwhile the pope with thirteen cardinals and large numbers of noblemen and incredible riches remained closed up in Castel Sant' Angelo. Since the Spanish could not take it by storm, they set a strong guard around it to prevent the pontiff and the cardinals from being secretly rescued at night. In order to protect the troops surrounding it, they began to lay out trenches, and they forced the most lowly of their prisoners and some of their own soldiers to dig them.

When news began to spread in Florence of the pope's disaster (even though it was suppressed for a few days), there was an immediate change in the confidence of those who were governing the state. The cardinal and Signor Ippolito began to fear and then to experience how difficult and dangerous it is in such a situation to control a population full of hatred and the memory of past offenses. Nonetheless they again persuaded themselves (as they had always done) that they could treat the people as harshly in bad times as they did in prosperity. With five thousand good soldiers in the city, well-paid and well armed, and others that could be hired very quickly, they showed their intention (as someone had advised them) to maintain their rule with violence and cruelty. Nonetheless, besides Signor Vitello Vitelli, who would not agree to march against the Palazzo della Signoria because he was paid by the senators, there were others among those whom they respected who were also in disagreement with this policy. These men desired the peace and health of the city even more than the interest and the honor of the Medici. They argued very convincingly that it was not possible to hold on to the state any longer by exiling and killing large numbers of people. But that it was better to try to rule the population with humane and civilized methods, and while maintaining the powers of the Medici, to give the people liberty. Realizing that almost all the citizens were up in arms, and that many people were fearlessly speaking out in public against the pope and his representatives, those who held the reins of power in the city on his behalf were undecided and confused.

Many people already showed clear signs that they were no longer willing to remain under the control of a government that they hated so much. Above all else they longed for the return of their natural and ancient liberty.

Even though Florence was in a state of shock and excitement, the cardinals there still had to consider ways to rescue the pope. Since his departure from Florence, the duke of Urbino had been repeatedly urged with the greatest insistence by the lieutenant-general to strike with all possible speed against the enemy. His Excellency, who had never broken stride since he heard that Rome had fallen into the hands of the imperial army, was still at Lake Trasimene. The lieutenant-general, the marquis of Saluzzo, and Signor Federigo da Bozzoli with the Swiss had, however, reached Orvieto. And so with still greater urgency, the duke was begged by the lieutenant-general and the cardinals and, once again in light of the pope's and the Church's peril, directed with great insistence to march swiftly to Rome. They argued that the imperial army was busy with its rich booty and obliged to guard a great number of prisoners besides, consequently it could not regroup itself and prepare quickly for battle. When His Excellency and his men appeared, it would be forced either to defend the eastern side of the Tiber (after cutting the bridges) or to retreat with the goods that had already been accumulated towards the kingdom of Naples. Nonetheless, neither these nor many similar arguments, which were repeated again and again by the lieutenant-general, the marquis of Saluzzo, and the Venetian quartermaster-general could persuade the duke to act against his own nature and will. The submissive and pitiful letters written to His Excellency by the pope and many of the cardinals under siege, which should have softened the hardest heart, did not make him change his plans at all.

In fact, when the duke's army should have been marching by the shortest route to Rome, they captured and sacked Castello della Pieve instead. Because it had refused to provide food to the army and lodging for the Swiss, they overran it and killed about seven hundred people. Then they turned towards Perugia, because the duke declared that it was necessary to restore Signor Orazio Baglioni to power and to dislodge Signor Gentile and his supporters, even though they had been put in power some time before by the pope. And after this task, which they easily achieved, having greatly lengthened their route of march with one excuse after another, they proceeded very slowly to the relief of Castel Sant' Angelo.

His Excellency was obligated to do this; the army had been promised again and again not only the opportunity to liberate those under siege in the castello, but also to recover the city of Rome, which it was eager to attempt. Finally, a few days later, they reached Orvieto. With no excuse to argue his customary difficulties and dangers, they halted with the intention of remaining in place until they determined the best way to aid the pontiff and where to camp safely near Rome. Federigo da Bozzoli (being more courageous and proud than the others) volunteered to attempt either to liberate the pope or to find a place for the army to encamp that would satisfy the duke. But Fortune (as people say) was entirely contrary to the pope's best interests. When Federigo was within a few miles of Rome with about 500 horse and 2,000 infantry, as he rode ahead of the army at a quick pace, without warning, his horse collapsed underneath him. He was so badly injured in the fall that he was carried dying to Viterbo.

When Francesco Maria learned of this, he apparently lost all hope of attacking the enemy, declaring that because of the reputation they had achieved, and because they were safe behind the walls of Rome, they could not be dislodged by force. If an attempt were to be made, it would be necessary to have an additional 15,000 infantrymen, and they had to be Swiss, because with any other nationality (as he had often stated) it would be impossible to defeat the imperial army. It was anybody's guess how His Holiness could hope to recruit these men, let alone pay for them, given that he was without money, without credit, and miserably trapped in Castel Sant' Angelo.

When Clement learned of the duke's opinion and his obstinacy about it, he finally understood, if he had not realized before, how terrible a mistake it was to have allowed his kingdom and his honor to be committed into the hands of such a cruel enemy. How wrong he was to have convinced himself that in Francesco Maria he would find that sense of responsibility and that respect that neither Pope Leo nor Lorenzo de' Medici nor indeed Clement himself had ever shown towards the duke.

What did Clement think would happen? His immediate predecessors had taken the duke's state and repaid the infinite benefits and good services he and his father had done for the duke of Nemours and all his offspring with ingratitude and cruelty. These were services offered at the very time, mind you, when the duke of Nemours was forced to beg for the means to live. Then the duke, by his own resources, and against the will of those who had ousted him, returned to power in his own state. When he was finally able to show the contempt and hatred for the Medici family that he had long nourished, was it likely that he would conceal it or give up before he saw that family entirely ruined and destroyed?

How many examples I could now bring forward to show that princes avenge the injuries they have received, if we didn't already have the example of Clement before our eyes. This pontiff erred extremely in entrusting his state and his honor to the duke. Ever since he became pope he showed that he had no less hatred for the duke than had Pope Leo or Lorenzo de' Medici. Even if no cruel act of vengeance is to be excused, I know of no other more defensible than this one, where there was so much malice on the part of Our Lord, and so much that is understandable and pardonable on the part of the duke. And if no one but His Holiness had suffered for it, or were going to suffer in the future, I would call it justice. This single example ought to be frightening enough to deter princes who cruelly and unjustly deprive not only whomever they happen to notice, but even those who have been their benefactors, of life and state without cause.

There is no doubt that if Francesco Maria had let the situation in which the pope found himself run its course until His Holiness himself acknowledged that his life and death were in the duke's hands, and then had liberated him afterwards out of his own virtue and generous spirit, that would be an example of humane and just revenge. But His Excellency lacked the supreme virtue that was possessed by Fabius Maximus and Sertorius. When Fabius Maximus learned that Minutius, who had insulted and defamed him many times, had been nearly destroyed by Hannibal, he came to his rescue and liberated him. When Sertorius' troops had attacked the enemy against his orders and were in great danger, he rescued them (as Plutarch tells) and let them go unpunished. But Francesco Maria, lacking such virtue, did only what served his vengeance, and it did not matter to him that everyone knew about an act that was so cruel and had such far-reaching consequences. Perhaps he thought that the magnitude of his revenge would win him glory, like the man who convinced himself that he could achieve lasting fame by setting fire to the marvelous Temple of Diana at Ephesus.

All the disasters and horrors of this war that have been described here from the very start resulted from the duke's hatred and malevolence. Because of this hatred, he allowed his army to sack and loot a large part of our territory in defiance of military order and even though we were in the same League, as if we were his enemies. With his permission, wherever his army passed, they left the words "FOR VENGEANCE" written on the walls of some palazzo. Because of this hatred, he has never helped the pope, nor will he aid him in the future; but where he can harm or damage the house of the Medici, he will never fail to do so.

I could spend more words and express this fatal error of Clement and the cruel conduct of Francesco Maria more effectively, if the screams and cries of the miserable prisoners tortured by the Germans and the Spanish, which continually resound in my ears, would allow me to think of anything but their terrible sufferings. I have decided therefore to describe these sufferings in detail, even though it was not the custom among past historians to write, except in general terms, about the misfortunes and disasters that occurred in captured cities. Nonetheless, in order that the rage of the victors and the process of divine justice be more clearly understood, I will describe the situation in whatever order is possible in such chaos.

My purpose is to show what sad and unlucky ends those governments come to which rule and maintain themselves in a culture of lust, greed, and ambition, rather than in military severity, beloved poverty, and just moderation. I confess that I cannot hold back my tears when I consider what torment and suffering human beings receive from their fellow humans, and how often we are the causes of our own misery and not Fortune (even though the majority of mortals blame her). Nonetheless I will force myself to describe some part of the pitiable events occurring in Rome in the very recent past.

So picking up where I left off, I note that after the Spanish and Germans had rested and recuperated somewhat from the incredible fatigue they incurred while scouring the city for booty, they began with many painful and cruel tortures to interrogate their prisoners. Their aim was to discover both hidden riches and the quantity of money their prisoners were able to pay for their liberation. Because they were pitiless and without respect for rank, sex, or age (like vile beasts), those whom they tor-

tured exposed their hiding places; and many, in order to
escape from present torture, agreed to ransoms so large
that afterwards it was impossible for them to pay. Those
who resisted and stubbornly refused to give the enemy the
designated sum endured intolerable sufferings worse even
than the unbearable fear of certain death. Indeed, they
experienced every conceivable form of suffering up to the
very point of death. And even though those who were
being tortured cried out continually for death, the cruel
and greedy Spaniards skillfully kept them alive, and there
is no doubt that they would have experienced much less
pain at the separation of their souls from their bodies.

If anyone had been walking through the streets of
Rome by day or night, he would have heard not sighs and
tearful laments, but the pitiful cries and screams of hap-
less prisoners coming from every house and building. For
they screamed in their suffering as if they were inside the
bull of Phalarus. The grandest nobles, the richest and
most refined prelates, cardinals, courtiers, merchants, and
Roman citizens who fell into their hands were all treated
more cruelly and with less respect in proportion to their
rank; and they tortured them with greater thirst for
ransom.

Indeed their hopes of becoming rich made them
torture such people more violently than others. Many
were suspended by their arms for hours at a time; others
were led around by ropes tied to their testicles. Many were
suspended by one foot above the streets or over the water,
with the threat that the cord suspending them would be
cut. Many were beaten and wounded severely. Many were
branded with hot irons in various parts of their bodies.
Some endured extreme thirst; others were prevented
from sleeping. A very cruel and effective torture was to
pull out their back teeth. Some were made to eat their
own ears, or nose, or testicles roasted; and others were
subjected to bizarre and unheard of torments that affect
me too strongly even to think of them, let alone to des-

cribe them in detail. Many cruel and pitiful examples were continually to be heard and seen.

Among many others the case of Messer Giuliano da Camerino, a courtier of the most reverend Cardinal Cibo, comes to mind. He was being tortured by the Spanish, who hoped to obtain an enormous ransom for him. Unable to bear the incredible torment any longer, he began little by little to approach the windows of the room were he was being held. When he saw his chance, he threw himself head first through one of the windows. When he hit the ground, he ended his life, his torment, and the outrageous demands of those who had hounded him so greedily.

There was another man named Giovanni Ansaldi, called Il Bacato, who was forced under torture to agree to a ransom of two thousand ducats. He was counting it out, when they began to torture him again, saying that they wanted to be paid in gold. Unable to bear any more pain, he threw himself at the man who was torturing him, and pulling this man's dagger from its scabbard, he killed himself. I could tell many similar stories, but I will refrain rather than dwell too long on such terrible things, especially since anyone can imagine on the basis of these two examples what the situation was like.

When in the midst of such horror these savages wanted to amuse themselves, using similar tortures, they would force the prelates and courtiers to confess to their infamous and criminal habits. The obscenity and filth of their actions not only amazed and stupefied the foreigners, but forced them to admit that they would never have imagined that the human intellect could conceive of such shameful and bestial things, let alone do them. For the sake of ridicule and punishment, they carried Cardinal Aracoeli one day on a bier through every street in Rome as if he were dead, continually chanting his eulogy. They finally carried his 'body' to a church where with great pleasure about half of his unusual (out of reverence, I will avoid saying 'criminal') habits were detailed in a funeral oration, along with those of other cardinals and prelates. Returning afterwards to his palace, they refreshed themselves in his presence with the finest wines voraciously drunk from consecrated chalices of gold. Later the same cardinal was seen in various parts of Rome as a prisoner, on some Spaniards back, in order to force him more quickly to come up with his ransom.

Our fellow Florentine, Bernardo Bracci, was on his way to the bank of Bartolomeo Velzieri with the light cavalrymen who had captured him. He had promised to pay them 7,000 ducats if they would spare his life. As they crossed the Ponte Sisto on their way to the bank, they ran into Monsignore della Motta, an officer of the imperial army, who asked them where they were taking the prisoner and why. When he heard the ransom they had agreed on, he said: "This is a tiny sum; if he doesn't add five thousand to it for me, throw him into the Tiber." So, to escape being thrown into the river – they had already set him up on the parapet of the bridge – he agreed to the additional ransom. And the whole sum was paid out by the bank.

A priest was shamelessly and cruelly killed because he refused to administer the most holy sacrament to a mule in clerical vestments. I will not describe what happened to the noble and beautiful young matrons, to virgins and nuns, in order not to shame anyone. The majority were ransomed, and anyone can easily imagine for himself what must have happened when these women found themselves in the hands of such lustful people as the Spaniards. Since they devoted such energy and skill to the task of making their prisoners pay incomparable sums of money in order to escape from their hands, it is probable that they applied the same methods in order to insure the satisfaction of their hot and intemperate libidos. Many are convinced that in this scene of outrage and terror, many noble and pure virgins, rather than fall into the hands of their lustful conquerors, stabbed themselves or leapt from some high point into the Tiber. I, however, have never heard that anyone has been able to positively identify a woman of such virtue and chastity. This should not be surprising considering how corrupt Rome is at present, how full of abominable vices and entirely lacking in the virtues it possessed in Antiquity.

I know that I am about to say things that many people will have difficulty in believing. Namely that the German and Lutheran soldiers, even though they are thought to be more inhumane and more prejudiced against the Italians than the Spanish, this time showed themselves to be more benign, less greedy, and much more tractable by nature than either the Spanish or Italian troops of the emperor. Many Germans, after the first furious wave of the attack was over, did not force their prisoners to undergo extensive torture, but they were content and satisfied with the sums of money that were offered freely. And many of them were both humane and respectful towards gentlewomen (even when they were young and beautiful). They brought them food and kept them at a distance from other prisoners, where they would not be insulted or injured by others. Consequently many prisoners at any early point in their capture, offering a small amount of money in comparison to what they could actually pay, were liberated without difficulty. This liberality and easygoing nature of the Germans is not to be attributed to their inexperience or to the fact that because they were very poor, every little offer of money seemed a lot to them. But it reflects a more humane and moderate nature. Certainly no one ever heard that the Spanish in their first raids, even though they were extremely poor, ever behaved towards their prisoners with such compassion and respect.

If it were not for the example of the other nationalities, I have no doubt, except for the prelates and clerics (these being the principal enemies of the Lutheran sect), the Germans would not have shown much cruelty against laypeople, either Roman citizens or foreigners. After hearing and seeing again and again, however, that in order to avoid torture, the prisoners of the other nationalities paid hundreds and thousands of scudi, and that many whom they had freed were secretly recaptured by the Spanish and then paid out huge sums of money to avoid torture; then they changed their nature and their methods. It is a common trait among people that they learn bad habits from each other more readily than good ones: especially when it is to their own advantage. And so after this the Germans exerted themselves to surpass every other nationality in the invention of barbarous torments.

One cannot imagine therefore an unbearable form of torture that their prisoners did not experience and endure many times for the sake of cruel and insatiable greed. How patiently these torments were borne by refined and delicate prelates and effeminate courtiers, is easy to imagine, if one realizes with what difficulty in good times, they bore, not the ills of the body, but the bite of a fly. And because many of these barbarians feared that their prisoners had not revealed to them all the money and valuables that they had hidden away, they forced their prisoners, even if they were high-ranking nobles, to empty with their own hands the sewers and other disgusting places where human excrement and the like were disposed of. Anyone can imagine how much pain and suffering that must have given to those who had always been accustomed to having their houses, their clothes, their bodies, and especially their boots perfumed with sweet and alluring scents.

It seems likely that this excrement with its ill effects on the vital spirits and its terrible stench, which was spread through every part of the city, would, along with the other disordered humors produced by so many months of suffering, cause plague. And indeed these vapors would be stronger and more poisonous, once they were heated up during the approaching summer. The effect would be to make a bad situation worse, and it would inevitably harm the victors as well as the victims. Meanwhile these victors lived it up enjoying everything to excess.

It was, of course, not always possible for them to identify those who fell into their hands, and it sometimes happened that nobles and rich men and women were able to liberate themselves after paying very small ransoms by pretending they were servants or other poor people. Whenever the Spanish happened to be fooled in this way, they would if possible have other men of their nation recapture these people; and so, many paid more than one ransom to liberate themselves. By pressing their prisoners on every side and finding huge treasures that had been hidden or buried in various places, in a very short time they became very rich. They came to set very little value on the clothing, pictures, sculpture, and other ornaments that they found, even if they were precious and of great intrinsic value. Objects of silver they also assessed at much less than their true worth. They set the highest value on beautiful jewels and pure gold, because they occupied little space and were easily recognized. So, when they sold a ring, for example (and this was often noted), they accepted a price based on weight alone because they attached no value to the pearls, diamonds, rubies, emeralds and other gem stones, some even engraved with perfect antique intaglios, which were set in them. Such stones were worth a great deal more by themselves than the soldiers were paid for the pure gold of the settings. Many unflawed ancient sculptures in marble and bronze, and medals of popes and prelates cast in various metals, which had been greatly prized for their workmanship and collected over long periods of time, fell into the hands of men who considered them worthless.

The immense riches of the Roman nobility, preserved in their families for many centuries, were destroyed in an hour. The incredible profits that had been accumulated and multiplied unjustly and dishonestly through years of usury, theft, simony, and other immoral means by courtiers and merchants fell in an instant into the hands of these barbarians. But why do I bother to recount the details of various fortunes or possessions that fell in such short time into the hands of these savage foreigners? Everybody knows that money, merchandise, and delicacies from all over Europe and much of the rest of the world came pouring into that city every hour to satisfy the insatiable appetites and the illicit desires of its many licentious prelates and courtiers. Because they had never feared that they might lose their possessions, the Romans were surprised, sacked, and slaughtered with incredible ease and enormous profit.

Those Germans, who had arrived only a short time before with Captain George von Frundsberg, now wore silks and brocades; huge gold chains hung across their chests and shoulders; and their arms were covered with bracelets inset with jewels of enormous value. Dressed up like mock popes and cardinals, they went for pleasure rides through Rome on beautiful hackneys and mules. Their wives and concubines, proud and richly dressed, accompanied them. The women's heads, necks, and breasts were covered with the largest pearls and the most perfect jewels pried from pontifical miters and sacred reliquaries. Their pages and servants were lustily and militarily dressed with various gashes and gores in their clothes. They had helmets of heavy gold and the barrels of their arquebuses were made of solid gold stripped from the altars and holy places of Rome. It would not have been possible to believe that these were the same people who had crossed the Po a few months before, after the disastrous and bitter death of Signor Giovanni, or entered the province of Romagna. Then they were exhausted, shoeless, and so poorly dressed that some of them were unable to keep even their private parts covered.

By the same token, no one would now recognize the cardinals, patriarchs, archbishops, bishops, protonotaries, generals, provincials, guardians, abbots, vicars, and all the rest of the ridiculous and infinite tribe of modern religious title-holders, who dishonor and burden the Christian religion. Now many of these men wore torn and disgraceful habits, others were without shoes. Some in torn and bloody shirts had cuts and bruises all over their bodies from the indiscriminate whippings and beatings they had received. Some had thick and greasy beards. Some had their faces branded; and some were missing teeth; others were without noses or ears. Some were castrated and so depressed and terrified that they failed to show in any way the vain and effeminate delicacy and lasciviousness that they had put on with such excessive energy for so many years in their earlier, happy days.

Not a few of these men could be seen taking care of the horses. Others turned the roasting spits and scrubbed the pots as scullery boys. Others carried wood, bedding straw, and water to their enemies and performed an infinity of other base services, as no doubt the majority of them had done before they acquired, through the exercise of wicked and shameful vices, the ranks they had never earned.

The sumptuous palaces of the cardinals, the proud palaces of the pope, the holy churches of Peter and Paul, the private chapel of His Holiness, the Sancta Sanctorum, and the other holy places, once full of plenary indulgences and venerable relics, now became the brothels of German and Spanish whores. And in place of the false ceremonies and lavish music, now you could hear the horses cough and neigh, and men cursing God and all the saints. They committed shameful acts on the altars and in the most sanctified places, in contempt of contemporary religion. Many sacred pictures and sculptures that had once been worshipped with vain ceremonies were burned and broken by iron and fire. Crucifixes were shattered by shots from arquebuses and lay on the ground; the relics and calvaries of saints lay among the dung of men and animals.

All the sacraments of the modern Church were scorned and vilified as if the city had been captured by Turks or Moors or some other barbarous and infidel enemy. There was no sin or villainy that these mad and impious Lutherans did not commit. When they saw the Germans dishonoring the churches and the most holy relics, the Spanish took this very badly; they began to curse the Germans, and they came very close to violence on this score. But in the end this disagreement was settled, and the situation quieted down; the Germans stopped destroying holy images and gave their full attention to tormenting their prisoners and revisiting the same houses. And the booty continually grew, since they always found something that had been hidden before but newly revealed by their prisoners.

I will not write of the anguish and confusion that those in Castel Sant' Angelo are enduring. With the pope, there are thirteen cardinals, innumerable prelates, lords, noblewomen, merchants, couriers and soldiers, all in terror and despairing of their safety. Since they are completely surrounded and very carefully watched by their enemies, I have little knowledge of what is going on inside. We can imagine, though (since they know that they cannot escape) that they spend their time blaming Jacopo Salviati, the datary, Signor Renzo, Cardinal Armellini, and perhaps the pontiff himself, in sharp and venomous words for their obvious and multiple mistakes. No doubt it is pointless, but many blame their own past patience; and there are many among them who could not be blamed if they took cruel and fatal vengeance on these men, before the eyes of the Holy Father.

One can easily imagine the anguish and torment of the pope, constantly seeing and hearing such a scourge of punishment raised against himself and against Rome.

Like the rest of those under siege, he is suffering in fear that he will soon fall into the hands of cruel enemies, obviously thirsting for his blood. And though he enjoyed great honors and sweet pleasures in the past, now he is paying for them with humiliation and pitiful distress. If he ever considered himself a wise and glorious prince, now he must acknowledge himself to be the most unfortunate and the most abject pontiff who ever lived. And since it is his fault that the Church, Rome, and Italy all find themselves in such extreme danger, we can easily imagine that he often looks toward the sky with tears in his eyes and with the bitterest and deepest sighs demands:

"Wherefore, then, hast thou brought me forth out of the womb? Oh, that I had died, and no eye had seen me!" [Job. 10:18]

THE END OF THE HISTORY
OF THE SACK
OF ROME
* * *
*

AFTERWORD

GUNPOWDER

HE RECURRENT INVASIONS of Italy that began in 1494 and reached their climax in the sack of Rome coincided with the introduction of gunpowder weapons. This was the greatest military revolution in history, and its impact has been exceeded only by the introduction of atomic weapons at the end of World War II. When cannon were first used against fortifications that had been built to withstand medieval siege techniques, the new weapons completely overwhelmed these traditional defenses. Within the first quarter of the sixteenth century, however, an entirely new style of fortification, which restored the balance between offensive and defensive weapons, was rapidly developing. Medieval fortifications, which were rigid, had been designed to deflect low-impact projectiles. Gunpowder-launched shot shattered such defenses. It was quickly discovered, however, that soft materials, like earth, absorbed the impact of shot, and sixteenth-century fortifications began to make immediate use of ditches and earthworks.

Since no specialized material was required, fortifications could and were protected against artillery very quickly. As a result of this adaptation of defensive structures to the new characteristics of offensive artillery, the tactics of siege warfare in the late 1520s were as conventional as they had been in the pre-gunpowder period. In fact the advantage, which had first yielded to the attacker armed with heavy artillery, seems to have passed back to the defender by the 1520s.

Even the threat of attack, however, brought devastating consequences for those outside the city walls. In order to make artillery fire most effective, the areas overlooked by the walls needed to be clear of obstacles. This necessity made the citizens of Florence fear even the threat of attack by Bourbon. The preparation of an unobstructed "field of fire" would require razing the many buildings in the suburbs of the city. Thus, whether the enemy burned outlying structures or they were razed to increase the effectiveness of defensive fire, the results were equally disastrous.

In Luigi's account it was the exception rather than the rule that fortified towns and especially cities could be overwhelmed and taken by besieging forces. Unless the fortifications of a town were undermanned, or the city was betrayed, attackers had very little hope. Where an attacking army had to fear counterattack while it was attempting to take a city by siege, there was very little likelihood that it would even try.

Because of the improvement in fortifications by the 1520s, heavy artillery played a very small role in the war Luigi describes. Gunpowder weapons, however, still had a great role to play, and the revolutionary implications of these weapons had hardly begun to be realized or exploited by 1527. The stable patterns of medieval warfare began to change when infantry weapons and formations became powerful enough to withstand cavalry attack. Gunpowder was only one of a number of innovations that changed the balance of power between infantry and cavalry. It did not at first even accelerate the slow shift away from a primary reliance on cavalry. English archers and Swiss pikemen had already shown that with the right kinds of weapons and formations, foot soldiers could defeat heavily-armored mounted knights. Bullets were not much better at piercing armor than arrows were, and early hand-held weapons took so long to load and fire that they required support from other traditional armaments to be effective. Men using small-bore artillery and hand-held guns joined the formations of soldiers armed with pikes and lances. These formed the mass that Luigi almost always refers to as *fanti,* "the boys."

The design of fortifications in the sixteenth century reflected not only the changes prompted by defensive measures against heavy artillery, but the use of gunpowder weapons against troops. The star and snowflake ground plans of Renaissance fortifications reflect the need to protect defenders from direct exposure to artillery fire. They also put guns and gunners in position to protect the fortification itself from approach by attackers. The aim of these structural elaborations was to provide flanking or "enfilading" fire from some portion of the structure on every square inch of outer wall. Any point that attackers might chose to undermine or assault must be covered by gunners from inside the fortress. The mathematical complexity of this problem was greatly increased by the geographical situations in which fortifications were placed, and the elaborate solutions to such problems were a source of interest not only to military experts but to men like Machiavelli, Leonardo, and Michelangelo.

While city walls were designed to defend against artillery and to place gunports where they could protect the walls against assault, they were not impregnable. Their circuits were so large, often, that they required substantial garrisons of troops to man them, and they passed over such irregular terrain in the case of large cities like Rome or Florence, that they were bound to have weak points. An attacker who found those weak points might eventually be able to overcome a walled city, especially if it was undermanned.

To protect and preserve the city's government and governor, even if the outer walls had been breached, there was often an inner fortification that played the role of the medieval castle or keep. Milan had such an inner fortress, as did Rome and many smaller cities in Italy such as Lodi. When the city of Milan was captured by Spanish troops in 1525, the duke, Francesco Sforza, and a large number of his supporters took refuge in the inner fortification there that is now called the Castello Sforcesco. For more than a year, while the rest of the city of Milan was entirely under the control of occupying troops, the Castello in its center remained impossible to capture. It was not until the summer of 1526, when food supplies within the Castello were finally exhausted that those within surrendered.

In Rome, the tomb of the emperor Hadrian (died 138 AD) was fortified in the new Renaissance style. Under its modern name, the Castel Sant' Angelo (*castel* is short for *castello*), it served as the inner fortress for the city of Rome, and when Rome was attacked in 1527, the pope, thirteen cardinals, and almost three thousand others took refuge there. While the rest of the city was in the hands of occupying troops, the Castel Sant' Angelo remained impregnable.

The most effective use of guns in 1527 was not against fortifications or masses of troops but at a distance and against individuals. Twice in the course of Luigi's history a sniper with his sights fixed on an enemy commander decisively affects the chain of events. The first and more devastating instance of the long-range effectiveness of gunpowder weapons brings down the Italian commander, Giovanni delle Bande Nere. Luigi presents him as the one man with sufficient courage, leadership, and strategic ability to defeat the imperial invaders. His death from a bullet wound promptly ended the counteroffensive he had launched against newly arrived imperial troops. Those very troops played a major part in the sack of Rome.

The second death is significant in a different way. This is the death, again by a sniper's bullet, of the imperial commander, Charles de Bourbon, before the walls of Rome. (In his celebrated *Autobiography*, the Renaissance sculptor and artillery amateur, Benvenuto Cellini, claims credit for this death, but his claim is implausible.) Bourbon had been the mastermind of the imperial attack on Rome. At first it appeared that his death, like that of Giovanni delle Bande Nere, would end the attack. In desperation, however, the subordinate officers of the imperial forces redoubled their efforts of attack and were ultimately successful despite Bourbon's death. Where his death is most significant, it appears, is in the events of the sack itself. When the Spanish and German troops gained control of Rome, they lacked the guidance and control of a supreme commander. Both George von Frundsberg, the leader of the German Lutherans, and Bourbon, the leader of the troops from Milan as well as overall commander, were dead. Had they been alive and commanding their troops once Rome was captured, events there might have taken a different, less anarchic, and less devastating turn. The Roman sniper who brought down Bourbon may have harmed his own cause much more than he impeded the imperial forces.

HEROES

 HESE TWO DEATHS throw into strong relief an aspect not only of Luigi's thinking about military affairs, but also an aspect of his style. Luigi never says the Venetian army did this, or the imperial forces did that. For the sake of making the text less alien to our own forms of speech I have often adopted that kind of short-hand expression. Luigi, however, always refers both to the army and its commander, even when the commander's role is not being emphasized. While we might say "the Third Army marched across the Rhine," Luigi would say, "General Patton with the Third Army marched across the Rhine." While this is in some sense a mere habit of phrasing, its continued use suggests a habit of thought. Luigi respects the rank and standing of commanders and his phrasing reflects this; but he also believes that commanders play the decisive role in the success or failure of armies.

In Giovanni delle Bande Nere and Bourbon, Luigi sees effective though dangerous leaders who can shape and motivate their troops and choose their battles with sufficient skill to practically guarantee success. Indecisive leaders, he believes, cripple their men. In fact it is the unsuitability for command of Francesco Maria della Rovere, duke of Urbino, that makes him the anti-hero of Luigi's history, a role that he shares with another great procrastinator and bungler, His Holiness Pope Clement VII. Clement, who is in effect commander-in-chief of the Italian forces, is, in Luigi's view, more to be pitied than blamed. Francesco Maria, however, receives less sympathetic treatment. This is partly due to the double game Luigi believed him to have played. It is also due to the duke's habit of shifting blame from himself and placing it on his troops. Luigi painted Francesco Maria as an enemy of the Italian soldier who was convinced that Spaniards or Germans were naturally and constitutionally better suited for warfare. This view was not only wrong but crippling and destructive, Luigi believed. It denied the hereditary connections between the Renaissance Italian and the Roman soldier in which Luigi strongly believed. It hamstrung any possible resurgence of Roman greatness through renewed military discipline, which was the heart of Luigi's social credo. An officer and his troops are interdependent forces, then, for good or ill, and Luigi never lets us forget the difference between them or their interdependency.

THE FORCE OF WAR

S THE POPE, beset by enemies both inside and outside Castel Sant' Angelo, laments his fate, Luigi abruptly ends his history. Its final scene is an image that epitomizes Luigi's understanding of his period. What more tragic low point than this could be imagined? Luigi views the pope's captivity and degradation as the worst situation that Rome, the Catholic Church, and Italy had experienced since the end of the Classical era. In his introduction, and again at the end of Book I, he expresses his hope that this low point will prove a turning point, and that in times to come Italian fortunes will begin to rise. He firmly believes that the story he has told can guide those who direct republics and principalities or advise their rulers as they seek this upward turn.

What does his history tell about the principles of European politics and diplomacy in the sixteenth century, and what does it reveal about violence and its management in Italy at that time? In my introduction, I reflected briefly on the parallel fates of the Aztec emperor and Clement VII. The humiliation and capture of both men occurred within the same decade, and, as Bourbon's speech suggests, some of the same soldiers may have participated in both. The two events are hard to contemplate at the same time, for one seems to unsettle and obscure the other. In Mexico, troops of the Holy Roman emperor attempt to wipe out entire races of New World people, and they oppose religious differences with outrageous force. Acts that appear to reflect religious outrage and deliberate genocide in the New World do not differ in kind from those carried out in Italy. Yet how can a mixed army of Spaniards, Lutheran and Catholic Germans, Italians, and maybe a few other nationalities be engaged in genocidal warfare in Italy? How can they wage a religious war against the spiritual leader of the faith they profess, for the most part, to revere? The way these armies wage war seems to be indifferent to the enemy they oppose. Luigi's account suggests that an army is a force in and of itself. It is difficult to recruit, to organize, and to direct. Once set in motion it is very difficult to restrain. Wherever it goes, it seems to follow the same unalterable program of devastation and outrage.

Limited, or what is now called "surgical," use of an army was nearly impossible in the Renaissance warfare Luigi knew, yet it remained an ideal. Desertion at all levels, failures of coordination, mutinies, and willful disobedience of orders were commonplaces. The continual failure of the duke of Urbino to pursue the war aggressively was a source of continual frustration to the pope and the Florentines. Bourbon's failure to obey direct orders to withdraw beyond the Po led to the sack of Rome. Food supplies, quartering, and wages were very uncertain. Bourbon's army lived off the population of Milan, commandeering their food supplies and extorting money from them to replace unpaid imperial wages. The truce negotiated between the pope and the viceroy of Naples entailed payment by Florence of the back wages of the very army that threatened it. One of Bourbon's arguments for the march on Rome was the eagerness of the Sienese to have this allied army off their hands. "Because we will be leaving their territory behind," Bourbon argues, "they will supply us more readily."

It is hard to imagine that so self-willed and imprecise an instrument could rationally be used in pursuit of the delicate balance of power that Italian political leaders worked to maintain. Their goal of neutralizing power by equalizing it led to the desertion of Charles V by his allies after the decisive French defeat at Pavia in 1525. The overriding goal of the Holy League, as Luigi presents it, was to counter the newly achieved imperial dominance in the Italian peninsula. This goal in turn dictated the focus of the offensive campaigns in the war.

In the north, the combined army of the League would attack Milan and attempt to restore Francesco Sforza to power. An Italian noble family with traditional claims on the government of Milan, but one that would be dominated by the French was to be reinstated. The kingdom of Naples would be attacked, primarily from the sea, by the armada of Andrea Doria. While the political goals in the north were very clear, those in the south were much less so. Luigi gives us no sense of whether the French would also be in the ascendancy in Naples, where they had traditional claims as well. The need to counterbalance the French might have dictated that even if the allies were successful, Naples should remain in imperial hands.

The halting conduct of the war in the north, plus the unexpected attack on Rome by Spanish and Colonna supporters put an end to the Holy League's offensive. Far from achieving a balance of power, the war of the Holy League exposed the allies to increased danger of imperial domination. As the imperial army moved out of Milan and gathered strength, their aim was a monopoly of power. The ideal of a balance of power no longer offered guidance even to the allies. They fell back on self-protection, more often at the expense of allies than of enemies.

While the war failed to restore the balance of power, it offered many opportunities to those who were lucky enough or powerful enough to exploit them. It is not surprising that a force with such devastating power would create new political conditions and opportunities almost at random. States and individuals seized the opportunities the war offered to realize private goals. As the imperial army made its way through central Italy, individual states in the Holy League ceased acting for the benefit of the alliance as a whole and increasingly pursued their own self-interest. Luigi accuses the duke of Urbino of positioning his army to protect Venetian territory only. Both the Venetians and the Papacy, Luigi charges, would prefer an attack on Florence to one on their own capitals. The Florentine and papal forces led by Francesco Guicciardini were deployed to protect Florence. While Luigi does not emphasize this, perhaps for obvious reasons, the successful defense of Florence sent the imperial army careening towards Rome.

Even secondary states along the imperial line of march tried to bend the army to their own political purposes. Siena clearly saw it as an instrument for weakening Florence and the Medici. Ferrara supplied the German lancers because they helped to weaken papal control over the territories at Ferrara's borders. Francesco Maria used his own army to oust the papally-imposed governors of Perugia, which was not in any sense a goal of the Holy League. In Florence, as Luigi repeatedly describes, many citizens saw the imperial army as a force to capitalize on in order to drive the Medici from power.

It may be banal to say that warfare had become a way of life in Renaissance Italy. The many political uses that communities and states tried to make of the armies passing through or near their territories suggest how well adapted these states had become to warfare as a political constant. People suffered from wars as they suffered from famines and plagues. All the same, warfare was a force that could be exploited. People kept their balance as best they could; they tried to avoid the worst consequences of warfare and to take advantage of its opportunities.

This was as true of those who declared or directed wars as it was of those who experienced them. Neither the pope nor Charles V had much directing control over the warfare made in his name. Each was prepared to take advantage of the benefits it offered him and was plausibly able to deny responsibility for its worst effects. Charles dissociated himself from the sack of Rome while reaping its benefits. Bourbon was an expert at exploiting the advantages of warfare. Luigi credits him with playing a masterful double game. At the very time he was asserting his obedience to the emperor, he was encouraging his officers and troops to resist the emperor's command. Yet neither the emperor nor Bourbon completely controlled the situation. Bourbon was continually frustrated in his efforts to move his troops out of Milan and unite them with the newly-arrived German lancers. Once these forces combined he was nearly killed by rebellious soldiers. Had Bourbon not been killed during the attack on Rome, he might have gone on in the style of Cesare Borgia to establish himself rather than the emperor as a major power in Italy.

Luigi's account underscores the notion that a territory devastated by war is not a place where normal diplomatic or policy conditions apply. This fact may impose the greatest limitation on the "surgical" or refined political use of warfare. A number of modern examples point to the same terrible conclusion: Somalia, Lebanon, the former Yugoslavia. The war of the Holy League grew out of the many wars that preceded it all the way back to the first French invasion of Italy in 1494. After thirty-two years of nearly continual warfare, the habits of soldiers, rulers, and citizens were strongly conditioned. In such a climate the idea of a "new" war that assembled new allies and set new goals was worse than fanciful. Like the perennial divisions between Guelfs and Ghibellines that had haunted Italy for centuries, the "new" war would inevitably resurrect old enmities. Limiting war among people and states who had become habituated to its conditions and opportunities would be equally difficult. Political leaders, officers, and soldiers were each going to look to the "new" war as an opportunity for satisfying old dreams.

Luigi does not present commanders as fully in command either of their armies or of the tactical situation. The more skillful commanders were those who knew how to take advantage of opportunities when they presented themselves. And of course warfare presented opportunities to common soldiers as well as to commanders. The events of the sack reveal this very clearly and suggest that the greatest suffering of warfare and the greatest opportunity for soldiers coincided. Ideals of warfare center on contact between armed combatants.[1] Luigi presents plenty of such actions but he also looks behind the veil drawn by other historians over the events that recurrently took place in a captured city. It is here that soldiers' actions were most appalling, and it is here that the greatest opportunities for enrichment and brutal self-satisfaction were to be found.

The imperial soldiers treated Rome as their own property. At first they slaughtered everyone they came upon, and Luigi depicts this as normal: in Book I he expressed his dissatisfaction with the allied failure to execute the imperial defenders of Cremona "as military custom required." After this initial rush, first the Spaniards and then the Germans began taking prisoners. Their aim was the accumulation of booty. They tortured their prisoners so that they would reveal hidden treasure and spur their friends and relatives to pay their ransoms. By all accounts, they were very successful in their endeavors. Individual officers and soldiers accumulated great sums of money. Carts of gold and precious objects rolled from Rome to Naples. Eventually some of the treasures of Rome must have ended up side by side with the gold of the Incas and Aztecs in Spanish coffers. Third parties with correspondents in Rome apparently made use of the sack to secure treasures for their art collections.

This is the abysmal low point that Luigi envisaged. He is too honest a chronicler, however, to obscure the fact that what was a low point for some was an opportunity for others. Perhaps this is the most timely lesson of the sack of Rome, that war is both ungovernable and rich in opportunities. Like the goddess Fortune herself, it grinds down and humiliates many, but it lifts others up, or at least offers them the promise of ascendancy. The dream of the condottiere; the dream of the common soldier ennobled, as Bourbon imagines him, by his commander;

the dream of the frustrated politician – all these center on war. Like Machiavelli's goddess Fortuna, war plays rough, and though she crushes many, she is sometimes mastered by strong, young, violent men.

Even Luigi, despite his age and experience, is not immune to her appeal. While he fears the political ambitions of a condottiere like Giovanni de' Medici, he cannot help but admire him. Undoubtedly the most interesting character in his book is Charles de Bourbon, Italy's arch-enemy. In addition to this continually awakened faith in (and fear of) strong men – which also applies to the book's dedicatee, Cosimo de' Medici, and to his overlord, Charles V – Luigi's historical philosophy itself embraced the devastations of war. If Italy were to rise again, Luigi appears to argue, it could only be from the ashes of her devastation. To be utterly destroyed by warfare may be the price and the key to her return to greatness. Tragically, like most of the political thinkers of his generation in Florence, Luigi appears willing to take that risk.

MONEY

HE SEDUCTIVE OPPORTUNITIES that warfare promised and the vast amounts of men and material it required made money a much more important part of the war-making endeavor than it had ever been before. While we tend to underestimate the role money played in medieval warfare, the general notion remains valid that feudalism supplied troops in a way that did not require huge cash outlays. In effect, feudalism bartered land for war power. In theory at least a vassal received his fief as a gift from his overlord, and in exchange he obligated himself to maintain and provide at need some contingent of fighting men. The money to equip and feed these men came from the agricultural surplus of the fief.

Renaissance armies whether national or mercenary received payment in money for their service. As William H. McNeill has shown, the levying of armies was an important step in the foundation of Renaissance, and hence modern, capitalism. He argues that:

> By collecting tax monies to pay soldiers who proceeded to spend their wages and thereby helped to refresh the tax base, Italian city administrations showed how a commercially articulated society could defend itself effectively.[2]

War was a very costly undertaking, and those costs were such that recourse to the banking system was essential if troops were to be paid. The imperial troops in Italy were, as Luigi repeatedly describes, not being paid by Charles V. When the war began, the troops stationed in Lombardy were already long overdue for their wages, and the payments that they received during the course of the war were all obtained through recourse to the financial opportunities warfare provided. These payments are seldom made to individuals as they generally were in the Middle Ages, but they were often collected systematically from a captive town (like Milan) and paid out to an entire army. By this means, warfare, which had always offered economic benefits to some individuals, now became, if it were successful, a self-financing venture.

Such ventures are of critical importance in the Renaissance. In the Middle Ages large public enterprises were financed through feudalism's channeling of agricultural surplus and through private donation and endowment. Over a period that may sometimes have amounted to centuries, a relatively modest portion of agricultural surplus could be systematically and effectively channeled towards a single goal. Raising a Renaissance army was nothing like building a medieval cathedral. The amounts of ready cash that military campaigns or programs of exploration demanded were enormous. Financing a levy of Swiss soldiers or a voyage to the New World, activities in which time was of the essence, required ready cash. The source a Renaissance ruler was most likely to turn to was an international banker. The cash once borrowed had to be paid back with interest, and pressure was placed immediately on the enterprise to become cash productive.

Luigi depicts the Spanish as avaricious beyond all limits. This gold hunger, however, is much more than an individual appetite or vice, it is an institutional need. What the Spanish were doing, whether in Italy or in the New World, cost a lot of money; and that money had to be repaid with interest, if possible by the enterprises themselves. That is what the Spanish attempted to do. In the Italian war and the sack of Rome both individual and institutional motives were working in tandem. The Empire was trying to recoup its outlay (or to pay for its troops without making a direct financial outlay), and the individual soldier was trying to enrich himself. The instrument both used was warfare with its opportunities for ransom and licensed plunder. When such activities were practiced by the mass of soldiers against alien populations the effects were devastating, and the financial gains substantial.

Banks participated in every aspect of this venture. They provided original financing for rulers who wished to raise armies, but they also provided ransoms and traded in promissory notes based on ransoms. It appears from Luigi's account that while Rome was being sacked and individuals raped and tortured, the banks functioned as usual. Soldiers do not appear to have robbed banks; instead, they extracted negotiable promises of ransom from their victims and cashed them in. This round-about approach shows the reliance that Renaissance soldiers placed on the particular opportunities for economic gain provided by the rules of warfare.

～

NOTES

1. See, for example, M. H. Keen, *The Laws of War in the Late Middle Ages* (London: Routledge & Kegan Paul, 1965).
2. William H. McNeill, *The Pursuit of Power: Technology, Armed Force and Society since A.D. 1000* (Chicago: University of Chicago Press, 1982), p. 78.

* *

*

Rom

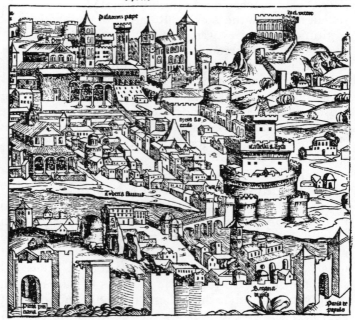

BIBLIOGRAPHY

Primary Texts and Contemporary Sources

Alberini, Marcello. *Ricordi*. Domenico Orano, ed. *Il Sacco di Roma del 1527: studi e documenti*. Vol. 1. Rome: Forzani, 1901.

Arborio di Gattinara, Mercurino (or Giovanni Bartolomeo da Gattinara). *Il Sacco di Roma nel 1527....* G. B. G. Califfe et al., eds. Geneva: Fick, 1866.

Aretino, Pietro. *Canzone*. "Deh, avess'io quella terribil tromba." (July 7, 1527) In A. Luzio, *Pietro Aretino nei primi suoi anni a Venezia e la corte dei Gonzaga*. Turin: Loescher, 1888.

——. *Frottola*. "Pax vobis, brigata." In A. Luzio, *Pietro Aretino nei primi suoi anni a Venezia e la corte dei Gonzaga*. Turin: Loescher, 1888.

——. *Lettere: Il primo e il secondo libro*. Francesco Flora, ed. 6: "A lo imperadore: Invito a liberare Clemente VII dopo il sacco di Roma"; 7: "A Clemente settimo: Esortazione al papa di non pensare a vendetta ma perdonare a Carlo V." *Tutte le Opere di Pietro Aretino*. Vol. 1. Milan: Mondadori, 1960.

Armellini, M., ed. "Gli orrori del saccheggio di Roma l'anno 1527 descritti da un cittadino romano di quel tempo." *Chronachetta mensuale di Scienze naturali e d'Archeologia* 4th ser., 20 (1886).

——. "Un documento del Sacco di Roma del 1527." *Chronachetta mensuale di Scienze naturali e d'Archeologia* 4th ser., 24 (1890).

Buonaparte, Jacopo (supposed author). *Il sacco di Roma. Ragguaglio storico attribuito a Jacopo Buonaparte*. Carlo Milanesi, ed. (See compilations below).

Cave, Jean. "Le sac de Rome (1527): relation inédité de Jean Cave Orléanais." L. Dorez, ed. *Mélanges d'archéologie et d'histoire de l'Ecole français de Rome* 16 (1896): 324-409.

Cellini, Benvenuto. *La vita da lui medesimo scritta.* G. D. Bonino, ed. Turin: Unione tipografico-editrice torinese (UTET), 1973.

Corsi, Paolo. *Ad humani generis servatorem in urbis Romae excidia P. Cursii civis romani deploratio.* Paris, 1528.

Giovio, Paolo. *Le vite di Leon Decimo et d'Adriano Sesto sommi pontefici et del Cardinale Pompeo Colonna scritte per Mons. Paolo Giovio vescovo di Nocera.* Lodovico Domenichi, trans. Florence: 1544.

Guicciardini, Francesco. *History of Italy.* Sidney Alexander, trans. and ed. Princeton, NJ: Princeton University Press, 1984.

—. *Storia d'Italia.* Emanuella Scarano, ed. Turin: UTET, 1981.

Macchiavelli, Niccolò. *The Chief Works and Others.* Allan Gilbert, trans. Durham, NC: Duke University Press, 1989.

—. *Lettere. Opere.* Vol. 3. Franco Gaeta, ed. Turin: UTET, 1984.

—. *Capitoli.* Giorgio Inglese, ed. Rome: Bulzoni, 1981.

Reissner, A. *Historia Herrn Georgen und Herrn Casparn von Frundsberg....* Frankfurt am Main, 1599.

Sanuto, Marino. *I Diarii di Marino Sanuto.* Vols 45, 46. Venice: 1896. Repr. Bologna: Forni, 1970.

Trivulzio, Scaramuccia. *Del sacco di Roma. Lettera del Cardinale di Como al suo segretario.* Carlo Milanesi, ed. (see compilations below).

Valdés, Alfonso (de). *Diálogo de las cosas ocurridas en Roma.* J. F. Montesinos, ed. Madrid: Espasa-Calpe, 1946. John E. Longhurst, ed. and trans. *Alfonso de Valdes and the Sack of Rome.* Albuquerque: University of New Mexico Press, 1952.

Vettori, Francesco. *Sacco di Roma. Dialogo.* Enrico Niccolini, ed. *Francesco Vettori scritti storici e politici. Scrittori d'Italia,* 252. Bari: Laterza, 1972, pp. 273-96.

MODERN COMPILATIONS OF ORIGINAL SOURCES ON THE SACK OF ROME

Lenzi, Maria Ludovico. *Il sacco di Roma del 1527. Strumenti* 89. Florence: La Nuova Italia, 1978.

Milanesi, Carlo, ed. *Il Sacco di Roma del 1527: narrazioni di contemporanei.* Florence: G. Barbèra, 1867.

Rodocanachi, Emmanuel Pierre. *La première Renaissance: Rome au temps de Jules II et de Léon X: la cour pontificale; les artistes et les gens de lettres; la ville et le peuple; Le sac de Rome en 1527.* Paris: Hachette, 1912.

Rodriguez-Villa, Antonio. *Memorias para la historia del asalto y saqeo de Roma en 1527....* Madrid: Imp. de la Bibl. de instruccion y recreo, 1875.

Scelta di curiosità letterarie inedite o rare 236. Bologna: Comm. per i testi di lingua, 1890. Includes *La presa e lamento di Roma, Lamento d'Italia, Lamento di Roma, Romae Lamentatio.*

SECONDARY SOURCES

Anselmi, Gian Mario and Paolo Fazion. *Machiavelli. L'Asino e le Bestie.* Bologna: Cooperativa Libraria Universitaria Bologna, 1984.

Biondi, Albano. "Tempi e forme della storiografia." Alberto Asor Rosa, dir. *Letteratura italiana.* Vol. 3. *Le forme del testo. II. La prosa.* Turin: Einaudi, 1984, pp. 1075-1117.

Chastel, André. *The Sack of Rome. 1527.* Beth Archer, trans. Bollingen Series 35, 26. Princeton, NJ: Princeton University Press, 1983.

Cochrane, Eric. *Florence in the Forgotten Centuries. 1527-1800.* Chicago and London: University of Chicago Press, 1973.

—. *Historians and Historiography in the Italian Renaissance.* Chicago and London: University of Chicago Press, 1981.

De Cadenas y Vicente, Vicente. *El saco de Roma de 1527.... Espana en Italia.* Madrid: Instituto Salazar y Castro, 1974.

Frutaz, Amato Pietro. *Le Piante di Roma.* Rome: Istituto di Studi Romani, 1962.

Giono, Jean. *The Battle of Pavia.* A. E. Murch, trans. London: Peter Owen, 1965.

Hale, J. R. *War and Society in Renaissance Europe. 1450-1620.* New York: St. Martin's Press, 1985.

—. *Renaissance War Studies.* London: Hambledon Press, 1983.

Hartt, Frederick. "Power and the Individual in Mannerist Art." *Studies in Western Art. Acts of the Twentieth International Congress of the History of Art.* Millard Meiss, gen. ed. Vol. 3. Princeton, NJ: Princeton University Press, 1963.

Hook, Judith. *The Sack of Rome.* London: Macmillan, 1972.

Jones, Rosemary Devonshire. *Francesco Vettori. Florentine Citizen and Medici Servant.* London: Athlone Press, 1972.

Keen, M. H. *The Laws of War in the Late Middle Ages.* London: Routledge & Kegan Paul, 1965.

Lee, Egmont. *Descriptio Urbis. Biblioteca del Cinquecento* 32. Rome: Bulzoni, 1985.

Lopez, Robert S. *The Three Ages of the Italian Renaissance.* Charlottesville, VA: University Press of Virginia, 1970.

Mazzei, Francesco. *Il Sacco di Roma.* Milan: Rusconi, 1986.

McNeill, William H. *The Pursuit of Power: Technology Armed Force and Society since A. D. 1000.* Chicago and London: University of Chicago Press, 1982.

Musto, Ronald G. "Just Wars and Evil Empires: Erasmus and the Turks." *Renaissance Society and Culture: Essays in Honor of Eugene F. Rice, Jr.* John Monfasani and Ronald G. Musto, eds. New York: Italica Press, 1991, pp. 197-216.

Oman, Charles. *A History of the Art of War in the Sixteenth Century.* London: Methuen, 1937.

Partner, Peter. *Renaissance Rome 1500-1559: A Portrait of a Society.* Berkeley, Los Angeles, London: University of California Press, 1976.

Pastor, Ludwig. *The History of the Popes from the Close of the Middle Ages.* 4th ed. Vols. 9-10. Ralph Francis Kerr, ed. and trans. London: Routledge & Kegan Paul, 1950.

Pepper, Simon, and Nicholas Adams. *Firearms and Fortifications: Military Architecture and Siege Warfare in Sixteenth-Century Siena.* Chicago and London: University of Chicago Press, 1986.

Phillips, Mark. *The Memoir of Marco Parenti.* Princeton, NJ: Princeton University Press, 1987.

Rossini, Giuseppe. "Il passagio per la Romgana delle truppe condotte da Carlo di Borbone al sacco di Roma (1527)." *Studi Romagnoli* 8 (1957): 269-77.

Sapegno, Maria Serena. "Il trattato politico e utopico." Alberto Asor Rosa, dir. *Letteratura italiana.* Vol. 3. *Le forme del testo II. La prosa.* Turin: Einaudi, 1984, pp. 949-1011.

Sasso, Gennaro. *Per Francesco Guicciardini, Quattro Studi. Istituto Storico Italiano per il Medio Evo, Studi Storici,* Fasc. 143-45. Rome: ISIME, 1984.

Schulz, Hans-Karl. *Der Sacco di Roma. Karls V. Truppen in Rom 1527-1528.* Halle: M. Niemeyer, 1894.

Stinger, Charles L. *The Renaissance in Rome.* Bloomington: Indiana University Press, 1985.

Taylor, F. L. *The Art of War in Italy 1494-1529.* London, 1921. Repr. Westport, CT: Greenwood Press, 1973.

* *
*

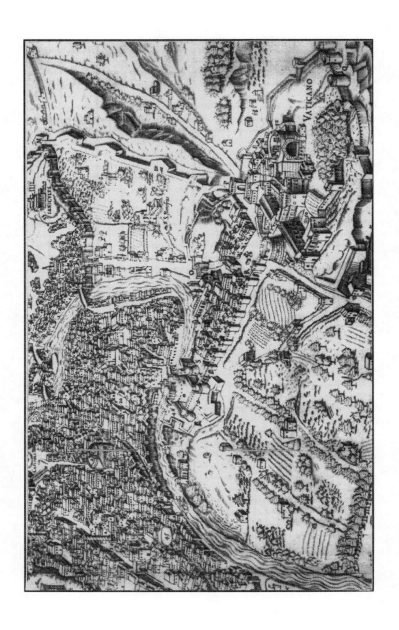

GLOSSARY

ARACOELI, CARDINAL see NUMAI, CRISTOFORO, CARDINAL.

ARMELLINI, CARDINAL: Cardinal Francesco Armellini de' Medici (1469-1527). Adopted into the Medici family by Pope Leo X; created cardinal 1517. Served as papal chamberlain and vice-chancellor under Clement VII. Reputedly avaricious and licentious.

BAGLIONI, MALATESTA (d. 1531): Member of ruling dynasty of Perugia and co-ruler of that city with his brother Orazio. Served as officer in Venetian forces. An implacable enemy of the Medici, he led Florentine forces against them in 1530, then betrayed Florence to its attackers. See also ORAZIO BAGLIONI.

BAGLIONI, ORAZIO: Member of ruling dynasty of Perugia. Served with his brother Malatesta as co-ruler of the city after 1527. Francesco Maria della Rovere turned aside from his march to aid the captive pope in May 1527, in order to drive Gentile Baglioni, a Medici partisan, from power and replace him with Orazio and Malatesta. Both brothers were sons of Giampaolo Baglioni, whom Pope Leo X had deposed and beheaded.

BANDE NERE, LE: Mercenary troops led by Giovanni de' Medici, also called Giovanni delle Bande Nere. The Bande Nere (literally "black bands") were black stripes on the armor and clothing of these troops originally worn in mourning for Pope Leo X.

BARBARIAN INVASIONS OF ROME: From the late fourth century AD, the Roman Empire and ultimately Rome itself were invaded by successive waves of tribes from eastern and northern Europe. The Visigoths sacked Rome in 410 AD, the Vandals in 455 AD. The sack of Rome in 1527 was often compared to these earlier invasions.

BLACK BANDS, see BANDE NERE.

BORGO: A borgo is a suburb of a city. In reference to Rome, "the Borgo" refers to the Vatican Borgo; the other major area so designated is Trastevere.

BOURBON, see CHARLES, DUKE OF BOURBON.

BRIAREUS: In his Dedicatory Letter, Luigi refers to Briareus as an example of human criminality, which was increasing as the Golden Age came to its end. Briareus, a hundred-armed Titan, is usually seen as the protector of Zeus. In his *Genealogie Deorum Gentilium,* however, Boccaccio describes Briareus as "contemptuous of Zeus and his enemy."

CAESAR: A common way of referring to the Holy Roman emperor, Charles V (q.v.). The term is preserved in the title, *Kaiser,* applied to the German emperor.

CAPUA, ARCHBISHOP OF, see SCHONBERG, NIKOLAUS VON.

CARPI, ALBERTO DA (1475-1550): Alberto Pio, Lord of Carpi. Wars in Italy frequently deprived him of control of his territories, which he finally lost in 1527. Served as French ambassador to the Papacy; in Castel Sant' Angelo with Clement during the sack.

CASTEL SANT' ANGELO: Mausoleum of the Roman Emperor Hadrian (d. 138 AD), converted to a fortress probably in the tenth century and connected to St. Peter's Basilica and the Vatican Palace by a covered walkway during the reign of Pope Nicholas III. Clement VII, thirteen cardinals, and some three thousand others took refuge there when imperial troops broke into Rome on May 6, 1527.

CERI, RENZO DA: Renzo dell' Anguillara, descendant of an important Roman family. Served with French forces in Marseilles; responsible for fortifications there that thwarted imperial attack. Papal officer and leader of defense forces in Rome in May 1527. Took refuge in Castel Sant' Angelo.

CESARINI, ALESSANDRO, CARDINAL (d. 1542): Created cardinal 1517. Adherent of imperial faction; refused to enter Castel Sant' Angelo with Clement and other cardinals.

CHARLES V, HOLY ROMAN EMPEROR (1500-1558): King of Spain as Charles I (ruled 1516-1556). Elected Holy Roman emperor, 1519. Son of Philip of Burgundy and grandson of Emperor Maxmilian I and Ferdinand and Isabella. Ruled Netherlands, Spain, Germany, parts of Austria, Sicily, southern Italy, and Naples. Cortez conquered Mexico (1519-21); Pizarro conquered Peru (1531-35) on his behalf.

CHARLES VIII, KING OF FRANCE (1470-1498): Invaded Italy in 1494 to reassert French claims to the kingdom of Naples. Began the period of wars and invasions in Italy culminating in the sack of Rome.

CHARLES, DUKE OF BOURBON (1490-1527): Also known as the constable or *connetable* de Bourbon (after 1515). Until 1523 an outstanding commander in the French army. After that date he gives allegiance to Charles V. Attempts invasion of France (1524). He takes part in the defeat of the French at Pavia (1525). Created duke of Milan in 1526 when Francesco Maria Sforza (q.v.) is deprived of his dukedom. Led imperial forces on their long march towards Rome; killed while attacking Rome.

CIBO, INNOCENZO (1491-1550): Nephew of Leo X and member of ruling dynasty of Genoa. Named cardinal, 1513. Important cardinal in court of Clement VII. Sent to Florence in winter of 1526-27 with Cardinal Ridolfi to strengthen Medici government.

CLEMENT VII, POPE, Giulio de' Medici (1478-1534): An illegitimate son of a Medici father, he was raised by his grandfather, Lorenzo the Magnificent. In 1513 his cousin, having assumed the papal throne as Pope Leo X, made him cardinal-archbishop of Florence. Throughout Leo's pontificate, the future Clement VII exercised great influence as an adviser. In 1523 he was elected pope with the support of Charles V. To restore the balance of power in Italy, he increasingly supported the French after their defeat at Pavia in 1525, a policy that culminated in the formation of the League of Cognac (q.v.) in 1526. From 1523 to 1529 Clement also governed Florence through intermediaries.

COLONNA FAMILY: Noble Roman family, prominent in church and political affairs after the twelfth century. Thirty members of the family became cardinals. One became pope as Martin V (ruled 1417-31). Despite connections with the Church, the family generally favored imperial policies and opposed several popes. A leading Guelf (q.v.) family; they held territories in the Roman Campagna and in the territory of Naples. Prospero Colonna (d. 1523) shared command of imperial troops in Italy with the marquis of Pescara (q.v.). Cardinal Pompeo Colonna (q.v.) opposed Clement VII.

COLONNA, CARDINAL: Pompeo Colonna (d. 1532). A leading candidate for the papacy in 1523, he was defeated by Giulio de' Medici, Pope Clement VII. Opposed Clement; led attack on Rome in 1526; encouraged imperial troops to sack Rome in 1527. Reconciled with Clement after the sack.

CONSTANTINE XI PALEOLOGUS (1404-1453): Last Byzantine emperor, killed in siege of Constantinople in 1453.

CONSTANTINOPLE: Modern Istanbul. Capital of the Eastern Roman Empire or Byzantine Empire. Conquered by Turkish forces under Muhammed II (q.v.), in 1453.

CORSINI, RINALDO (1487-1547): Member of Florentine mercantile and political family with members supporting the Medici and others, like Rinaldo, a leader of the 1527 uprising, who were hostile to them.

CORTONA, CARDINAL (OF), see PASSERINI, SILVIO.

COSIMO DE' MEDICI (1519-1574): Son of Giovanni delle Bande Nere and Maria Salviati. Descendant of both the elder and cadet branches of the Medici family. Second duke of the Florentine Republic (1537), after the assassination of Alessandro de' Medici; first grand duke of Tuscany (1569). Luigi Guicciardini dedicated the *History of the Sack of Rome* to him (after 1537).

CURIA, ROMAN: The cardinals and other high officials of the Roman Catholic Church form the court or *curia* of the pope.

DATARY: The papal datary maintained a private treasury entirely in the control of the popes that assumed great importance in the Renaissance as an independent economic resource. See also GIBERTI, GIAN MATTEO.

DIANA, TEMPLE OF, AT EPHESUS: The Temple of Diana or Artemis at Ephesus was, according to a widespread classical legend, burned by one Herostratus for no other reason than to achieve fame.

DORIA, ANDREA (1468-1560): Genoese admiral and statesman. Commanded French fleet against Charles V (1524-1528). In the War of the Holy League, his ships blockaded Genoa and attacked imperial sea-ports serving Siena and Naples.

EMPEROR, see CHARLES V, HOLY ROMAN EMPEROR.

ENCKENVOIRT, CARDINAL WILLIAM VAN (1464-1534): Born in the Netherlands; created cardinal in 1523; papal datary under Pope Hadrian VI. Favored imperial cause and so did not seek sanctuary in Castel Sant' Angelo at the time of the Sack of Rome; held for ransom by Spanish troops. Later aided in the reconciliation of pope and emperor (1529).

FABIUS MAXIMUS: Roman general and dictator. During the invasion of Italy by Hannibal, Fabius maintained contact with the enemy but would not trust his troops to an open engagement. Minucius denigrated this policy and rashly attacked Hannibal; he and his troops were rescued by Fabius. The story is told in Plutarch's "Life of Fabius."

FERRARA, DUKE OF: Alfonso I d'Este (1486-1534). Under feudal obligations to both pope and emperor, he sided with Charles V and aided imperial troops in the winter of 1526-27. Alfonso was the third husband of Lucrezia Borgia. Great artists of the Renaissance were patronized at their court, including Ariosto, Bembo, and Titian.

FRANCIS I, THE MOST CHRISTIAN KING OF FRANCE (1494-1547): King of France after 1515. He made repeated attempts to capture and hold territory in Italy. In 1525 his army was defeated at Pavia by imperial troops, and Francis was captured and imprisoned. Released from prison in 1526, he repudiated the Treaty of Madrid and joined the League of Cognac. His support of the war, however, was minimal.

FRANCESCO DEGLI ANGELI, FRIAR, see QUINONES, FRANCISCO DE.

FRANCESCO MARIA DELLA ROVERE, Duke of Urbino (1490-1538): Grandson of Federico, duke of Urbino, he was adopted by his uncle Guidobaldo and succeeded him as duke in 1508. He served another uncle, Pope Julius II, as captain-general of papal forces. Leo X, the first Medici pope, removed him from his dukedom in 1516 and replaced him with a Medici. After Leo's death, Francesco Maria recovered his dukedom but apparently continued to nurture a hatred for the Medici. He fought with the Venetians against the French and was named captain-general of Venetian forces in 1524. In this capacity he served in the army of the League of Cognac.

GENOA: Ligurian port city. In the period of the League Wars, it was in the hands of imperial forces. It was blockaded and nearly captured by Andrea Doria (q.v.).

GENTILE, SIG. = GENTILE BAGLIONI, see BAGLIONI, ORAZIO.

GERMANICUS: Surname of several Roman generals who gained victories over the Germans, especially Nero Claudius Drusus Germanicus and his son, Germanicus Caesar.

GHIBELLINE PARTY: The Ghibelline faction or party was allied with and supported the emperor.

GIBERTI, GIAN MATTEO (1495-1543): Governor of Tivoli until named papal datary by Clement VII in 1524. Pro-French and instrumental in winning Pope Clement's adherence to the League of Cognac.

GIOVANNI DE' MEDICI (1498-1526): Son of Giovanni di Pierfrancesco de' Medici (also called Giovanni Popolano) and Caterina Sforza. Given a minor military command by Pope Leo X in 1516, by 1523 he had achieved considerable power and reputation. Served the imperial army and the French at various times, always as leader of his Black Bands (q.v.). He was fatally wounded while fighting German lancers in the area south of Mantua during the war of the Holy League. Giovanni was the father of Cosimo I de' Medici, the first grand duke of Tuscany and the dedicatee of Luigi Guicciardini's *History of the Sack of Rome*.

GONFALONIERE FOR JUSTICE: Chief executive officer in Florence serving a very restricted term. Luigi Guicciardini held this office in April and May of 1527.

GONFALONIERE OF COMPANIES: The organizer but not necessarily the commander of a militia unit in Florence.

GRAND TURK, see SULEIMAN I.

GUELF PARTY: The Guelf party or faction was allied with and supported the Papacy.

GUICCIARDINI, FRANCESCO (1483-1540): Younger brother of Luigi. Lawyer, military and political leader under the Medici. During the War of the League of Cognac, he served as lieutenant-general of papal forces. Wrote *History of Italy*, published posthumously.

HOLY LEAGUE, see LEAGUE OF COGNAC.

HORATIUS COCLES: A Roman who, according to legend, held off the Etruscan army from the wooden Sublician bridge in Rome until it could be demolished.

IPPOLITO DE' MEDICI (1509-1536): The elder of two Medici heirs taking part in the government of Florence 1524-27. The cardinal of Cortona, Silvio Passerini (q.v.), acted as regent for the two young men. Bypassing Ippolito, Clement installed Alessandro as duke of Florence in 1532. Ippolito died of poisoning in 1535. Alessandro was assassinated by his cousin in 1536; he was succeeded by Cosimo de' Medici (q.v.)

JANUS: A Roman god of beginnings, often represented as a two-faced head. Guicciardini's association of him with the Golden Age is based on his appearance at the beginning of Ovid's *Fasti*.

JERUSALEM: After four years of resistance to Roman attack, Jerusalem fell in 70 AD to forces led by the Roman general Titus.

LANNOY, CHARLES DE (1487/88-1527): Childhood friend of the future Charles V (q.v.); he was a member of his council after 1515. In 1522 he was named viceroy of Naples and so became governor of Sicily and the southern half of Italy; he was thus the chief imperial officer in Italy. Active in imperial campaigns in Italy from that date. He negotiated a peace treaty with Clement VII in 1527 and tried unsuccessfully to convince Bourbon to accept it.

LEAGUE, see LEAGUE OF COGNAC.

LEAGUE OF COGNAC: Alliance of France, England, Venice, Florence, Francesco Maria Sforza (deposed duke of Milan), and the Papacy against Emperor Charles V.

LEVA, ANTONIO DE: Imperial officer. Lieutenant of the marquis of Pescara (q.v.). Commanded forces defending Pavia against French, 1524-25. Commanded imperial troops opposing League of Cognac, 1526-27.

LIEUTENANT-GENERAL, see GUICCIARDINI, FRAN-CESCO.

MANTUA, MARQUIS OF: Federigo Gonzaga II. Under feudal obligations to both the pope and emperor, he nominally sided with the latter but aided the League. When German lancers marched into Mantuan territory, he urged them to enter the area south of the city, known as the Seraglio of Mantua (q.v.), where they were hemmed in by the Po and Mincio rivers. Here they were nearly trapped and destroyed by League soldiers.

MIDAS: Legendary king of Phrygia granted the ability to turn everything he touched to gold. He serves as a symbol of avarice, one of the faults that accompanies the end of the Golden Age.

MOMUS: In Greek myth a personification of "blame."

MONCADA, DON UGO OF (1476-1528): Spanish nobleman and soldier. Fought repeated battles in Italy. In

1526 he attempted to prevent the formation of the Holy League. During the war that followed, he led a contingent of Spanish troops and participated in the surprise attack on Rome and sack of 1526. During and after the sack of 1527, he negotiated with the pope on behalf of the emperor. On the death of Charles de Lannoy (q.v.), he became viceroy of Naples.

MOST CHRISTIAN KING OF FRANCE: Guicciardini usually refers to the king of France as *Cristianissimo* = Most Christian. The epithet is conventional after the mid-fifteenth century. In 1527 this was Francis I (q.v.).

MUHAMMED II (1430-1481): Sultan of Turkey, called "the conqueror" or "the great." Besieged and captured Constantinople in 1453, thus putting an end to the Byzantine Empire.

NAPLES, KINGDOM OF: The kingdom of Naples comprised Sicily and most of southern Italy as well as the territory surrounding its principal city. Until the mid-thirteenth century it was ruled first by the Normans and then by the Holy Roman emperor. The French house of Anjou won control of it at that time, but lost it to the Spanish in 1442. At the time of the sack of Rome, the kingdom of Naples was ruled by Viceroy Lannoy (q.v.). It served as a refuge for the Colonna (q.v.), the Guelfs (q.v.) and as a staging area for Spanish attacks on Rome.

NEMOURS, DUKE OF: Giuliano de' Medici (1479-1516). Third son of Lorenzo the Magnificent. When his eldest brother, Pietro, was deposed as ruler of Florence, Giuliano joined him in exile. They were aided at first by the duke and duchess of Urbino, parents of Francesco Maria della Rovere. When the second of Lorenzo's sons, Giovanni de' Medici, became pope as Leo X, he ousted Francesco Maria from his duchy and made his nephew Lorenzo (1492-1519), duke in his place. Luigi sees this act of ingratitude towards the duke of Urbino and his father as the motivation for Francesco Maria's acts of revenge against the Medici.

NINUS: Legendary founder of Nineveh. Husband of Semiramis. According to legend, she killed him and usurped his throne introducing a reign of unrestrained libertinism. Guicciardini associates Ninus with the decline accompanying the end of the Golden Age.

NOFRI, PIERO: Captain of Florentine Infantry.

NUMAI, CHRISTOFORO, CARDINAL (d. 1528): Member of Franciscans and high office holder in the order. Created cardinal 1517, and most often referred to by his titular church, the Aracoeli. Despite his Ghibelline views, he was roughly treated by imperial soldiers during the sack and probably died from injuries suffered at that time.

ORSANMICHELE: Florentine church in the vicinity of the Piazza della Signoria. In the abortive uprising against the Medici, which Luigi describes, it served as headquarters for the Medici while they negotiated with those occupying the Palazzo della Signoria.

PALAZZO DELLA SIGNORIA: Seat of Florentine government, taking its name from the Signoria (q.v.) or chief executive council of Florence. It has been known since the late sixteenth century as the Palazzo Vecchio.

PASSERINI, SILVIO (1459-1529): Cardinal of Cortona, 1517. Medici supporter, he governed Florence (1524-1527), as regent for Ippolito (q.v.) and Alessandro de' Medici. His dictatorial style of government contributed to the ouster of the Medici in 1527.

PESARO, PIETRO: Venetian quartermaster-general. Member of leading Venetian patrician family, he served as chief supply officer in the army of Francesco Maria, whose policies he often opposed.

PESCARA, MARQUIS OF: Ferrante Francesco de Avalos (1489-1525). Spanish, born in Naples. Commander-in-chief of imperial forces in Italy; fought at Ravenna (1512), Milan (1521), La Bicocca (1522), Pavia (1525). At Pavia captured the French king, Francis I. Giovanni Morone, an agent of Francesco Maria Sforza (q.v.), duke of Milan, attempted to convince him to betray his allegiance to Emperor Charles V. When Pescara exposed the plot, Morone was executed and Sforza deprived of his dukedom.

PHALARIS: Tyrant of Acragas in Greek Sicily, remembered for his cruelty; he is supposed to have roasted his enemies alive in a bronze bull.

PICCOLOMINI, GIOVANNI, CARDINAL: Cardinal of Siena and imperial adherent; did not take refuge in Castel Sant' Angelo with Clement.

QUARTERMASTER-GENERAL, VENETIAN, see PESARO, PIETRO.

QUINONES, FRANCISCO DE (1475-1540): Francesco degli Angeli, created Cardinal Santa Croce (1527). Franciscan who acted as mediator and negotiator between Clement and Charles V both before and after the Sack.

RANGONI, COUNT GUIDO (d. 1539): Illustrious officer, served first in the Venetian army, then under Leo X. Florentine officer under Clement VII.

RIDOLFI, NICCOLO, CARDINAL: Nephew of Leo X and supporter of Medici political ambitions. Sent along with Cardinal Cibo (q.v.) in the winter of 1526-27, to Florence by Clement VII to shore up government of Ippolito de' Medici and Cardinal Passerini (q.v.).

SALUZZO, MARQUIS OF: Michele Antonio (d. 1528). Hereditary ruler of Saluzzo and surrounding territories in the area between Lombardy and the Alps. Active as French commander in the Italian wars as early as 1513.

SALVIATI, JACOPO: Member of a leading Florentine family with close ties to the Medici and Guicciardini, Jacopo married the sister of Leo X, served as Secretary to Clement VII, and was with him in Castel Sant' Angelo.

SANTA CROCE, CARDINAL, see QUINONES, FRANCISCO DE.

SARDANAPOLIS: Greek form of the name Asurbanipal, last Assyrian king. A symbol of extravagance, tyranny, and willfulness.

SCHONBERG (or SCHOMBERG), NIKOLAUS VON, ARCHBISHOP OF CAPUA: (1472-1537) Dominican, created cardinal 1535. Served in curia of Clement VII, where he actively promoted imperial policies.

SCIPIO AMELIANUS AFRICANUS: Roman general responsible for the destruction of Carthage in 146 BC, the conclusion of more than one hundred years of warfare between Carthage and Rome.

SERAGLIO OF MANTUA: An area southeast of Mantua tightly bound in by the Mincio and Po rivers. German lancers were at risk of being trapped here but escaped, crossing the Mincio at Governolo after the death of Giovanni de' Medici.

SERTORIUS, QUINTUS (d. 72 BC): Distinguished Roman general. Luigi repeats an anecdote from his life narrated by Plutarch in his "Life of Quintus Sertorius."

SFORZA, FRANCESCO MARIA (b. 1492): Made duke of Milan by Charles V in 1522. Forced from his throne at the time of the French occupation in 1524. In 1525, he attempted to turn Pescara (q.v.), the imperial commander in Italy, against the Emperor Charles V. The plot was discovered and the emperor deprived Sforza of his dukedom. In 1526, the dukedom was granted to Charles, duke of Bourbon (q.v.). Sforza took refuge in the Castello in Milan, while the city was occupied by Spanish troops. Relief of the duke and his reinstatement was a principal aim of the Holy League (q.v.). In 1526, Sforza submitted. He was reinstated by the terms of the Treaty of Bologna (1530).

SIENA, CARDINAL, see PICCOLOMINI, GIOVANNI, CARDINAL.

SIGNORIA: The chief executive council of Florence. The Signoria met in the Palazzo della Signoria (q.v.) in the piazza of the same name.

SULEIMAN I: The Magnificent (1496-1566). The "Grand Turk." Became Turkish sultan in 1520; conquered the island of Rhodes in 1522; invaded Hungary and threatened Austria (1526).

TITUS: Roman general, son of Emperor Vespasian, conquered Jerusalem in 70 AD. On his triumphal arch in Rome, important ceremonial objects from the temple in Jerusalem are depicted.

TRIVULZIO, SCARAMUZZA, CARDINAL (d. 1527): Named cardinal by Leo X, 1517. Lobbied for French interests in the papal court.

USELESS MOUTHS: Noncombatants in a town under siege. As food supplies diminished, they were often forced outside the walls.

VALDARNO: The Arno River valley in the area both upstream and downstream from Florence.

VASTO, MARQUIS OF: Alfonso de Avalos d'Aquino. Nephew of Pescara (q.v.). Took over command of his forces at his death.

VESPASIAN: Roman emperor, 69-79 AD, began campaign against Judea, which was brought to its conclusion by his son Titus.

VISTARINI, LUDOVICO: Member of important noble family of Lodi. Served imperial interests in Italy. Perhaps moved by severity of Spanish occupation in 1526, conspired to open Lodi to soldiers of the League.

VITELLI, VITELLO (d. 1528): Officer first in Venetian forces, then in the service of France and the Papacy. Succeeded Giovanni de' Medici as commander of the Bande Nere.

* *
*

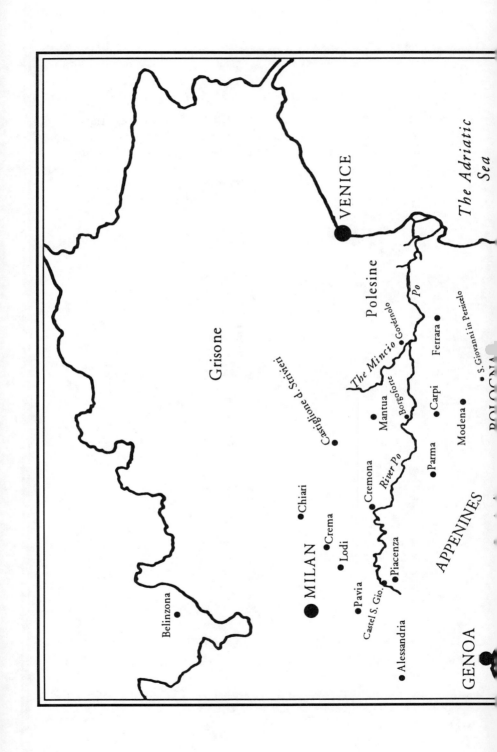

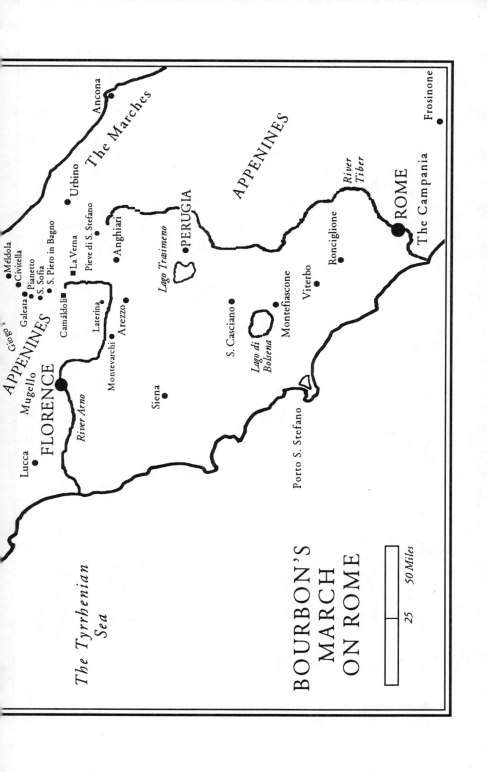

BOURBON'S
MARCH
ON ROME

The Tyrrhenian
Sea

Lucca •
FLORENCE
River Arno
Mugello
APPENINES
Giogo
Camáldoli ■
Laterina •
Montevarchi •
Arezzo •
Siena •

Méldola •
Galeata • • Civitella
S. Sofia • Pianetto
• S. Piero in Bagno
■ La Verna
Pieve di S. Stefano •
• Anghiari
Lago Trasimeno
• Urbino
The Marches
Ancona •

APPENINES
• PERUGIA

APPENINES

S. Casciano •
Lago di
Bolsena
Montefiascone •
Viterbo •
Ronciglione •
River
Tiber
ROME ●
The Campania

Porto S. Stefano •

Frosinone •

25 · 50 Miles

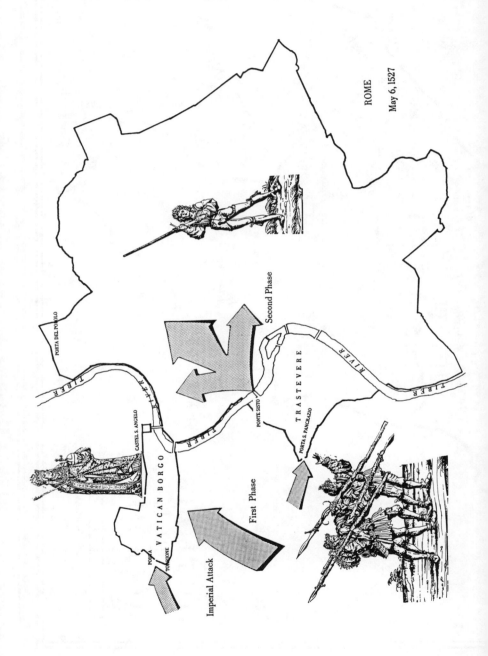

ROME
May 6, 1527

This Book Was Completed on October 12, 1992 at
Italica Press, New York, New York and Was
Set in Garamond. It Was Printed on 50 lb
Booktext Natural, Acid-Free Paper
with a Smyth-Sewn Binding
by BookCrafters,
Chelsea, MI
U. S. A.
* *
*